HORROR PATRIAE

HATJE
CANTZ

The Return of Toxic Nationhood

~~steirischerherbst'24~~

Edited by
Ekaterina Degot
and
David Riff

Contents

9

Introduction: The Return of Toxic Nationhood

Ekaterina Degot and David Riff

Twenty twenty-four will be remembered as the year nationalism made a spectacular comeback to the political stage. The electoral victories of far-right parties in European elections and the triumph of Donald Trump's reelection bid in America are only the tip of the iceberg. The entire political discourse has shifted, possibly for decades to come. Tribalism, particularism, local pride, and national self-consciousness have flooded all sides of the political spectrum, to the point that they influence one another and become hard to discern.

Much of this change has been a long time coming and is difficult to characterize merely as a shift to the right. Ever since the 1990s, the Left has mediated its formerly universal agenda for social justice through grievance-based politics of identity that often turned into a "Victimhood Olympics" between competing oppressed minorities. From the mid-2000s onward, the far right has been taking over this lexicon of grievance, using it to channel the resentments of the silent majority. Its electoral agendas consist in protecting the endangered white species from immigrants and phantom communists and making their purportedly cancelled identities "great again."

Such a renewed "greatness" of nations and empires would have been unthinkable not long ago. For at least two decades after the end of the Cold War, it might have seemed that empires and nations were eroding, or, at least, that peaceful coexistence would be the ultimate fate of all countries. This might be what gave Benedict Anderson the necessary critical distance and irony to write *Imagined Communities*, describing the half-fictional construction of national identities.[1] It was this book, written in the last phase of the Cold War, that formed the point of departure for the 2024 edition of steirischer herbst festival.

For Anderson, nations arose in the wake of universalizing, supranational empires—a form partially rehabilitated during the Cold War with the standoff of two universalizing projects. The collapse of socialism (as a universalistic postnational empire) also entailed the erosion of its twin, the Pax Americana. It was especially the linkage between postnational free market trade and liberal democracy that seemed increasingly hollow, given new inequalities.

Eventually, the national community appeared as an illusory refuge. Under Vladimir Putin, Russia was reinvented as a national empire, intent upon territorial expansion, and now the US under Trump seems poised to follow suit. Imperial and expansionist thinking is not only the domain of new national empires—the People's Republic of China is another example—but also of smaller countries. Some of Benjamin Netanyahu's messianic ultranationalist coalition partners dream of establishing a Greater Israel (including not only the West Bank and Gaza, but also parts of Syria and Lebanon), admired in Europe by right-wing politicians. Meanwhile, another universalizing project, the EU, edges ever closer to falling apart, with small nationalisms arising to assert themselves against its influence and that of the larger nation-empires.

If there is a common denominator between nationalisms large and small, it is probably frustration and resentment, which feed into an attack upon existing institutions, elites, and expert knowledge. Public institutions left over from the age of social democracy are under siege, and the Left struggles to protect them, thrust into a conservative position. The assault and the demand for revolutionary change now come from the Right—fueled by the grievances of silent majorities.

It is with this feeling in mind that we created steirischer herbst '24, *Horror Patriae*, whose exhibitions, performances, and discussions tackled the questionable and uncanny histories of nostalgic and imaginary constructions of nationhood, juxtaposed with neglected and silenced stories of strange encounters, hybrids, and happy miscegenation—to oppose the claim of purity. This dense program is documented in a richly illustrated catalogue.

The focus of this edition was very much on Austria and Styria, where the ultraright Freedom Party (FPÖ) won both federal and state elections, leveraging the "small" nationalisms of both country and region while normalizing mild xenophobia. The celebration of local culture comes with a hidden imperial dream of attaining former greatness, but also with a deep sense of foreboding, inner contradiction, a darkness from the past that cannot be denied. There is a profound feeling of nonbelonging right in the middle of what is supposedly home, and that was one of our chief focuses in the program.

In addition to its yearly catalogue, steirischer herbst also publishes an annual reader of essays and literary texts. This year, we aimed for an incisive collection of texts about the rise of new nationalisms, traditionalism, and communal patriotisms and how to resist them. What seemed crucial was to provide space for a new analytical and distanced language for current developments. In the maelstrom of today's renewed culture wars, it seems that precisely such a distance is the scarcest commodity.

Sociologist Thorsten Mense has been observing the return of national rhetoric to the German political scene for nearly a decade now. In his contribution, he describes how the untranslatable term *Heimat*, or homeland, has gained near-universal approval, with an uncanny absence of critique of its history as a Nazi battle cry. Mense catalogs the horrifying and partly comic instances of how *Heimat* became an advertising slogan and a means of selling politics across the political spectrum. These include the Left in places such as Thuringia, which did not help to stave off the rise of radical right-wing parties, but rather helped to further shift the paradigm of politics at large.

Mense argues that patriotic sentiment and connected notions such as *Heimat* not only immobilize their subjects, binding them to one place, but that they are inextricable from violence and exclusion. "*Heimat* can only have value in a world in which millions of people are forced to flee," he writes. Mense sees "a progressive answer to the reactionary longing for natural belonging" in identifying with rootlessness of the kind described by émigré philosopher Vilém Flusser as a form of freedom.

In his contribution, Anton Jäger questions recent interpretations of the Right's electoral successes. There is a long tradition, stretching from 1920s Marxist theorist Karl Korsch to Didier Eribon, of attributing them to a "switch" of working-class electorates from socialist to neo-nationalist, populist parties—one that could be reversed. Jäger challenges this idea, highlighting the role played by frustration and apathy, and not some new sublimated energy.

Outwardly, Jäger argues, the Right successfully appears as "hyperpolitical." But unlike historical fascism, it is not intent upon building durable institutions. There is no real program, aside from keeping the migrants out. This offers a stark expression of deep contradictions at the heart of European financialization, whose spoils angry voters are demanding to get their share of. As Europe's prosperity has depended so heavily on migrant labor, anti-migrant agendas appear as purely self-destructive gestures. These are born of a general dissatisfaction with liberalism at large, which does not mean that liberalism's left-wing rivals are asking the right questions. To Jäger, there is "no 'energy' [in Europe's extreme-right surge] that can be recuperated," but rather a universal frustration that has material roots and needs to be addressed.

One of the most troubling elements of the New Right's global strategy is the instrumentalization and weaponization of antisemitism, which is supported by Israel's most right-wing government ever. Especially in Germany, this plays a crucial role, leading to a decisive change in the entire political climate. In his contribution, Ingo Niermann provides a darkly ironic history of German guilt, its invention, and subsequent elevation to a part of the German raison d'état.

Niermann argues that despite its anti-totalitarian and anti-racist intentions, inherited guilt for the crimes of World War II has itself become a branch of identitarian and *völkisch* ideology, according to which a special sense of guilt is what makes Germans unique if not superior. Niermann looks at how this ideology grew out of the German identity crisis that beset it after reunification, and how it was installed as an alternative to a faltering European identity. He argues that collective ascriptions of guilt or victimhood are ultimately homogenizing, exclusionary, and fascistic. What is needed is a means of redistributing historical guilt.

What went wrong and why did postnational projects falter? Why did the nation-state and its constructed collective identity return? Philosopher Boris Buden rereads Benedict Anderson's *Imagined Communities*, honing in on the vast differences between our time and the time in which it was written. As Buden argues, Anderson idealizes the consolidating power of national languages, while ignoring the tendency toward standardization, the inequalities between languages, or the impact of digitization and English as a new lingua franca.

Precisely these forces have eroded the vernacular national languages and communities that 19th-century nations were built upon, and there is no way back, Buden argues. Today's commonalities and shared languages reach across national borders. The nations of today, he argues, are "zombies," while the so-called West is "the ventriloquist of its afterlife." The new nationalisms "evacuate the fictional center of the national community—where the old one had imagined its cultural substance—and move to its borders," which now become sites of struggle for imagining commonly owned global languages and defying their foreclosure.

In her contribution, philosopher Keti Chukhrov offers a very different view of the so-called West and how it plays into local history, also challenging how Western commentators look at purportedly non-Western contexts. Looking at examples from dance and music, she questions the dominant (critical) view of Western modernity as kinetic, disciplined, composed, individualistic, and fundamentally hostile to the Global East or South. Rather, Western theorists have classically misread non-Western cultures, failing to recognize kindred elements and disregarding the actual complexity of these cultures.

Ultimately, it is hybridity and mutual cultural appropriation that make up culture, especially in the non-Western world. Chukhrov cites the example of Georgia, part of the Arab world for centuries and under the influence of its translations from Greek, but also an extension of Byzantium. She argues that culture, art, and poetry can be products of such pressures and at the same time above them, attaining a new form of universality.

The reader concludes with two conversations about the current impact of the global political shift to the right and its local implications. Theater director and head of the Vienna Festival Milo Rau joins steirischer herbst director and chief curator Ekaterina Degot to discuss the looming questions of censorship as well as the differences between Western complacency and the recent developments in Eastern Europe.

Writer and curator Ranjit Hoskote joins steirischer herbst senior curator David Riff to discuss the cultural backgrounds of the persistent rightward shift in India and its alternative, a possible cosmopolitics. As Hoskote argues, a trans- and nonnational culture is possible, and it exists in cultures of translation. Under present conditions, these are hard to maintain, but worth fighting for and recuperating.

1 Benedict Anderson, *Imagined Communities: Reflections on the Origin and Spread of Nationalism*, rev. ed. (London: Verso, 2006).

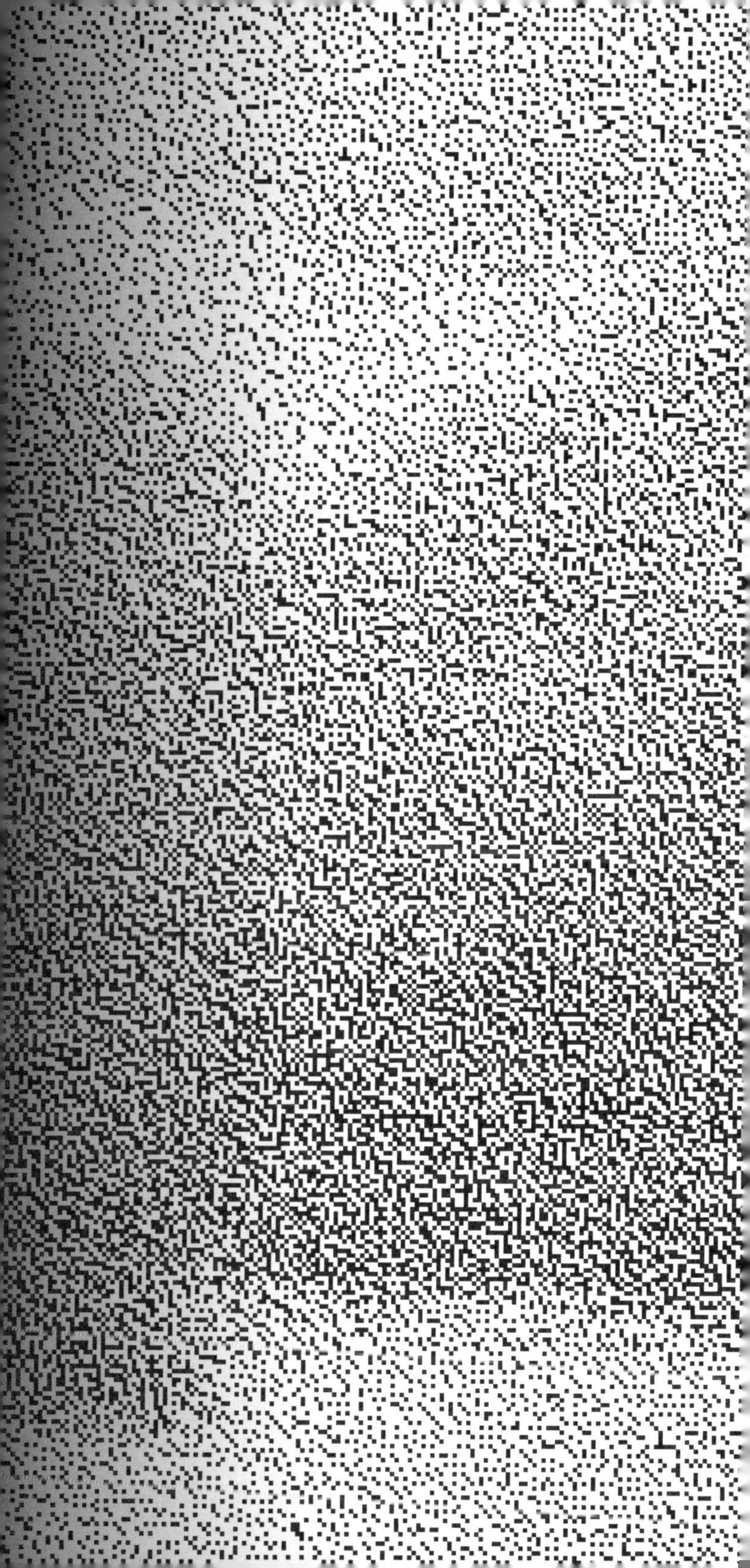

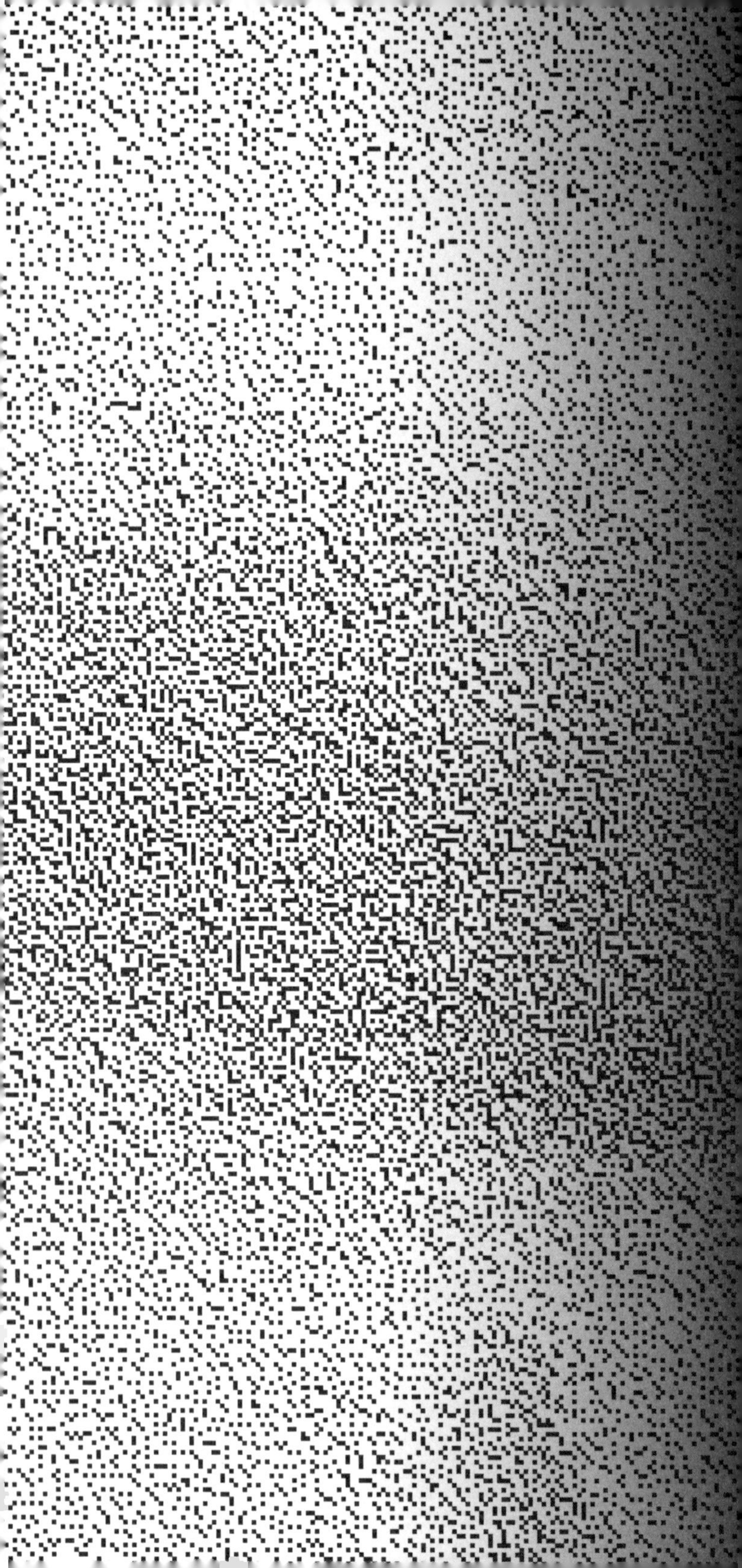

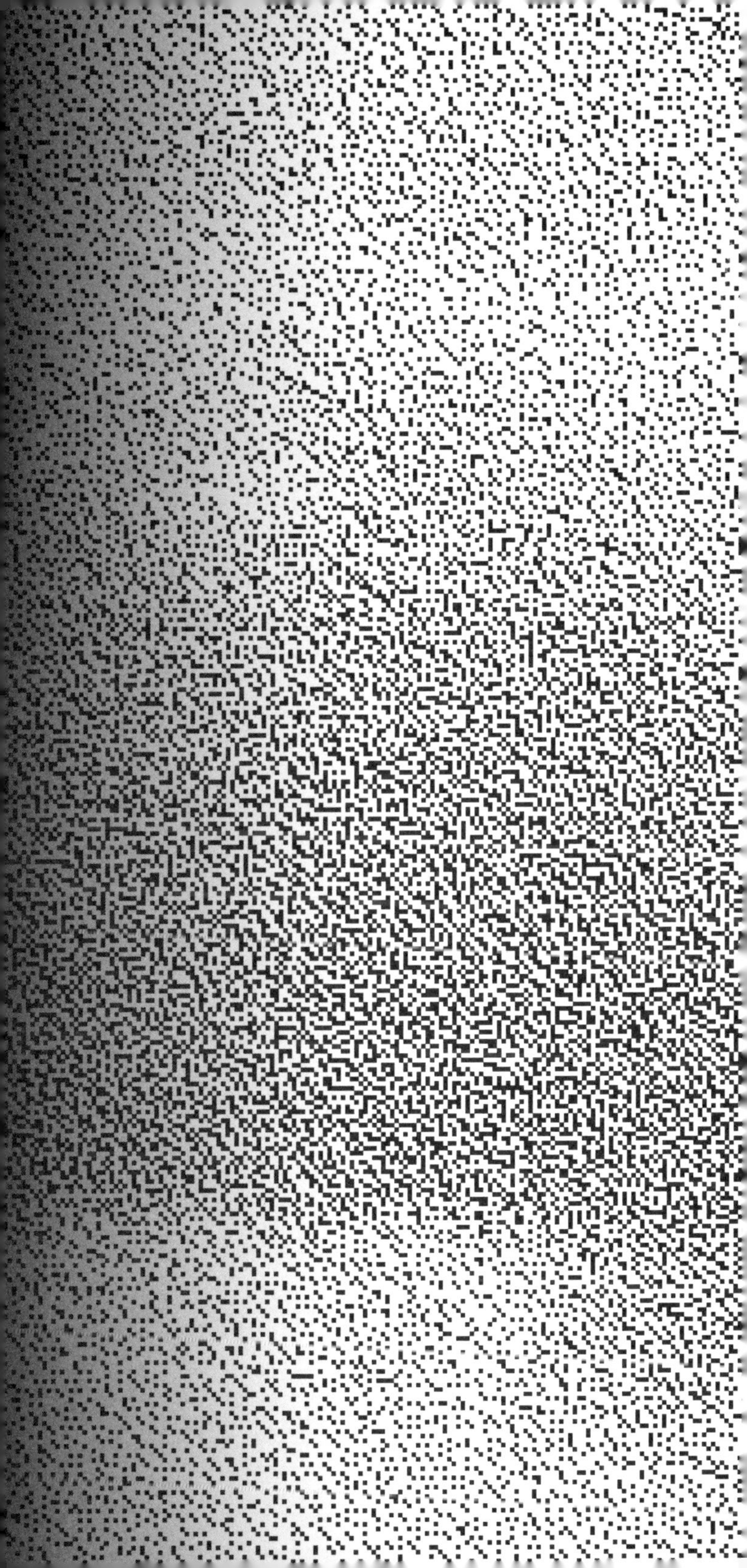

Thorsten Mense

There Is No *Heimat*

25

Heimat is everywhere. There is no escaping this untranslatable German term, which lies somewhere between "home," "homeland," and "fatherland" semantically.

From Greenpeace to the supermarket chain Hofer, from the Freedom Party of Austria (FPÖ) to the Greens, from the Federal President of Germany to the Identitarian movement—everyone loves it, wants to fight for it, preserve it, protect it, and defend it. At least since 2017, a real *Heimat* boom has taken Germany and Austria by storm.

The absurdity, arbitrariness, and extent of this newly discovered love of *Heimat* is astonishing. We have learned that *Heimat* is "the smell of bratwurst" as well as "the moon that accompanies the wayfarer at night," but, most importantly, "a good feeling," as we can hear on the radio and read in magazines. Greenpeace tells us that "*Heimat* needs environmental protection," while the neo-Nazi National Democratic Party of Germany (NPD) claims that "environmental protection is *Heimat* protection." Supermarket chain Kaufland wants us to "rediscover our *Heimat*" in their stores.

Extended debates in the culture pages, hour-long radio features, and photo competitions were the hallmarks of the boom's early days. In his 2017 German Unity Day speech, Federal President Frank-Walter Steinmeier said *Heimat* nineteen times in thirty minutes. Five years later, in Austria, his counterpart Alexander Van der Bellen proclaimed, "Those who love their *Heimat* do not tear it apart," thereby helping him to win the presidential election.

Heimat has become a quintessential political battle cry. Its specific connotations are defended in books, debates, political and cultural committees, funding programs, street protests, and attacks on refugee shelters. The *Heimat* boom in politics and media comes with an unprecedented mobilization of pop culture. In 2018, a book bearing *Heimat* in its title was published on average every day in Germany, with a total of over four hundred. And *Volks-Rock 'n' Roller* Andreas Gabalier, wearing lederhosen while singing about *Heimat*, plays in sold-out stadiums.

What is even more surprising than this craze is the conspicuous absence of its critique. While there is a feverish debate on what constitutes *Heimat* and how it can be identified, hardly anyone seems to question the concept itself, the "feeling" and the longing for natural belonging it implies. Despite all superficial differences, everyone agrees on one point: *Heimatlosigkeit* (a lack of *Heimat*, a "home[land]lessness") is an existential deficiency or even a mental disorder.

In the past, such notions and forms of regressive collectivity and naturalizing communitization always faced radical and uncompromising criticism from the Left, while the liberal bourgeoisie was at least careful with terms such as *Volk* and *Nation*. In the case of *Heimat*, all reason seems to have been suspended. Surveys indicate that over 80 percent of Germans view the term positively.[1] Where are suspicion, skepticism, and negation to be found when everyone wants and, above all, feels the same thing?

A Right-Wing Concept

Almost all those involved act as if *Heimat* had always been close to their hearts. This is a blatant lie, as the concept barely featured in political discourse until a few years ago. It is easy to pinpoint the moment when it arrived: in 2017, when the "social *Heimat* party" FPÖ was preparing to enter another coalition in Austria, while in Germany, the Alternative for Germany (AfD)—according to its then-chairman Alexander Gauland, the "only true party of the *Heimat*"—rose to become a serious political contender. *Heimat* thus comes from the Right. They run election campaigns with it, dedicate long sections of their party programs to the concept, incorporate it into the name of their organizations, produce hashtags and T-shirts. The racist murderers of the National Socialist Underground (NSU), who killed ten people between 2000 and 2007, emerged from the militant neo-Nazi group Thüringer Heimatschutz (Thuringian Homeland Protection), and the racists who, since 2015, have demonstrated against refugees and for border closures in Cottbus call themselves Zukunft Heimat (Future Homeland). The AfD wants to "give the *Heimat* a future," which, as can be seen on their election posters, means "consistent deportation" and razor wire around Germany. In June 2023, the NPD even renamed itself Die Heimat. For right-wingers and neo-Nazis, *Heimat* and ethnic homogeneity are identical.

The fact that *Heimat* is and historically always has been a Nazi battle cry does not sit well with those who want to save the *Heimat*, protect it from alleged right-wing abuse, and drag it out of the fascist morass. Such thinking is familiar from debates on the nation, and yet the zeal and vehemence with which it is contested is astounding.

On German Unity Day in 2017, President Steinmeier said: "We must not leave this longing for *Heimat* to those who construct *Heimat* as an 'us versus them,' as nonsense about blood and soil."[2] Among the first to agree with him was the then-leader of the German Greens, Cem Özdemir, who praised "the fact that the federal president is putting the concept of *Heimat* in positive terms and not leaving it to those who badmouth our republic and divide our country."[3] For Bodo Ramelow, a member of Die Linke (the Left Party) and former prime minister of Thuringia, the *Heimat* "is not something that some Nazi could ever take away." He dismissed any critical reflection on the matter in advance: "That's where I draw the line."[4]

As always, to avoid giving right-wingers a monopoly on right-wing notions, the Left adopts them, thereby making them appear harmless and aiding their reactionary spread. Just a few years ago, the Identitarian movement chanted "Love of *Heimat* is not a crime!" and saw this as an oppositional stance—which was not entirely wrong. Today, this slogan no longer meets with any objections. On the contrary, a rallying cry such as "We love this country! It is our *Heimat*! We will fight for this *Heimat*!" does not need to come from the Identitarians, but can, as in this case, also stem from a former parliamentary leader of the Greens, Katrin Göring-Eckardt.[5]

From rather open-ended discussions on whether to save people lost at sea in the liberal weekly *Die Zeit* to conservative, purportedly democratic politicians openly questioning the Geneva Refugee Convention and the right to asylum, public discourse has shown just how much has become negotiable. Meanwhile, Germany's traffic light coalition has reintroduced border controls, thus implementing a key demand of all right-wing extremists in recent decades.

The extension of what Germans felt they could say and do had already begun in 2006 with the outbreak of party patriotism during the FIFA World Cup, celebrated as an opportunity to finally feel proud as a German and of Germany again. "Mut zu Deutschland" (Courage for Germany) was also the slogan used by right-wing extremists to enter the Bundestag eleven years later. The self-redemption of the Germans—which Eike Geisel described in *Die Wiedergutwerdung der Deutschen* (How the Germans Became Good Again)[6]—during the 2006 "summer's tale" prepared the ground for the massive spread of ethnonationalism in the shape of the AfD. "Preserving *Heimat*" was their other slogan for the 2017 federal elections. Today, the *Heimat* has its own ministry, and the fascists fight the Greens over whose love for it is greater and truer.

A Soundtrack for *Völkisch* Mobilization

The *Heimat* boom is the ambient rumble of a society moving to the right. It not only shows how right-wing terms have been adopted and normalized in public discourse, but also reveals a widespread reactionary desire for natural affiliations, authenticity, and a return to origins. For years, sales of traditional clothing have been rapidly increasing. The most widely read consumer magazine (apart from TV guides) is the "bloom-and-soil" lifestyle publication *Landlust*, while *Heimat* festivals and projects are springing up everywhere, generously funded by the state.

It is the task of criticism to reveal the underlying social causes, because this need for *Heimat* is fueled by real experiences of isolation, alienation, loss of self-determination, and social disintegration. It is an answer by subjects to the repressive conditions constantly afflicting them. Those who seek to escape by looking for a *Heimat*, however, are not out to change the world, but rather to reconcile themselves to the circumstances. It is an escape that can only lead to its opposite.

Heimat is the wrong answer to societal conditions gone wrong. The debate about it obscures the material causes of alienation and involves the depoliticization of social issues. Suddenly, everything is *Heimat*, whether the talk is fiber optic rollouts, the improvement of local transport, affordable housing, a sufficient pension, or the conservation of the environment. When expressed as mere social demands, these claims no longer seem justified. And if rents continue to rise, pensions continue to fall, and the bus still doesn't reach the village, then blame the foreigners who don't care about our homeland. Talk of a "globalist class" and a "rootless elite" barely conceals antisemitic resentment. Even the Left Party harps on about the rivalry between autochthones and immigrants.

The splinter party Sahra Wagenknecht Alliance (BSW) is quite open to the question of identity and, as is the rule, thus also to racism. In the fall of 2024, during its state elections campaign in parts of eastern Germany, the party promised that it would "give a *Heimat*" to everything (dignity, education, peace, health)—except, of course, to migrants, against whom it stoked hatred in a way no different from the AfD. In return, the BSW received over 10 percent of the votes in its first elections.

Heimat stands for a modernized version of the *Volksgemeinschaft* (racial community), a new edition of familiar debates about people, nation, and identity. That's how people are prepared for all the unreasonable and inhumane things to come. It is no coincidence that the German debate about *Heimat* began in 2015, the so-called summer of the refugees. An effort to develop a concept of society (and not community[7]) corresponding to a postmigrant reality together with the newcomers—whose number, anyway, is negligible—has never been made. Rather, the aim is to close ranks on the home front. Once again, the Germans have set out to find themselves. It is a quest that should be of great concern to those who may not belong to them.

Left-Wing Love of *Heimat*

Many on the left refuse to recognize the reactionary and violent potential of *Heimat* and are thus unable to prevent regressive notions of community from taking root. When Medico International, Kritnet, and the Institut Solidarische Moderne tried to mobilize the remnants of so-called civil society against the refugee policy's increasing barbarity with the slogan "solidarity, not *Heimat*," they were reprimanded by their comrades: it should be "solidarity and *Heimat*"—ignoring that the conjunction allows the slogan to become part of every far-right rally. Even I felt the wrath of left-wing *Heimatschutz* when I published a critical article in the daily *Neues Deutschland* titled "Ein brutales Gefühl" (A Brutal Feeling).[8] Not only do many on the left not want the Right to take away their *Heimat*, they are even less willing to accept leftists who express reservations about this authoritarian formation of a new German national identity.

Instead, Christoph Türcke, a would-be critical theorist, demanded and published a "rehabilitation" of the concept as early as 2006.[9] Sahra Wagenknecht maintains that *Heimat* is "not a right-wing term."[10] Diether Dehm, on the other hand, a member of the Left Party and proponent of a *Querfront* (a loose alliance of the far right and far left based on national populism), asked in *Neues Deutschland* in late 2018: "Don't all people have a right to a homeland protected from the terror of free trade, with regional trade flow, social security, and no war?"[11] Whoever writes such a thing must know that "free-trade terror" and war are necessary—far away from one's own corner of the world. This is the only way the homeland can be spared.

Like Dehm, Bodo Ramelow also considers it a serious mistake that the Left is unable to relate to the concept of *Heimat*. He is proud of the fact that he promoted traditions in Thuringia more than any other prime minister before him. Ramelow was in office from 2014 to 2024: economic growth was stable, exports and wages were rising, and unemployment fell to 5 percent, the lowest since reunification. The proportion of foreign citizens is equally low: 4.7 percent.

For many Thuringians, who are doing rather well according to the numbers, this is still too much. More than half of them, 58 percent, believe that Germany is "in danger of being overrun by foreigners," as shown by the University of Jena's *Thüringen-Monitor*, published in November 2018.[12] Forty-nine percent believe that migrants only come to Germany to exploit the welfare state. Four years earlier, this figure was still at 36 percent. Now, the Leipzig Authoritarianism Study shows similar results for all of eastern Germany.[13] However, it is striking that approval of various aspects of "xenophobia" is 5 to 10 percent higher in Thuringia than the eastern German average while the state is better off economically than its neighbors.

Since the red-red-green coalition took office in 2014—the first of its kind in the country at the time—xenophobic and racist attitudes in the free state have risen steadily and massively, in some areas by as much as a third. Why? The *Thüringen-Monitor* cited above offers possible answers: in Thuringia, love of one's homeland is even more widespread than in the rest of Germany (96 percent stated that their *Heimat* was "important" or "very important" to them), and the stronger the love of one's homeland, the greater the resentment of migrants: "A sense of attachment to one's *Heimat*, ideas of an exclusive community of residents, and the exclusion of 'strangers' are connected," the study concludes.[14]

Ramelow refused to see this correlation and instead insisted: "If someone sees their *Heimat* as a shelter, then they should have that shelter."[15] This is a dangerous promise because the study unequivocally shows what it is that people want their *Heimat* to shelter them from. The fall 2024 election results confirmed this equally clearly: in Thuringia, a far-right party, the AfD, won a state election for the first time since the end of Nazism.

Left without a Home

Obviously, attempts by members of civil society and the Left to use the longing for *Heimat* for their ends pursue a different agenda than the nationalists. Not everyone who calls for *Heimat* is shouting “Foreigners, go home!” That said, such attempts do require a subtle but unyielding critique. In this regard, Michael Scharang is absolutely right: “The old whining about the homeless left is pathetic. A left that has a homeland is no left at all.” With this, he refers to the well-known quote from Jean Améry: “Left, where there is no *Heimat*.”[16]

As beautiful and concise as this sentence is, Améry’s relationship to home was much more dialectical: “You need to have a home in order not to need one,” he wrote in his 1966 essay “Wieviel Heimat braucht der Mensch?” (How Much Homeland Does a Person Need?).[17] Today’s leftists are only too happy to point to this and similar statements by left-wing intellectuals to justify the longing for home as a deeply human, innate feeling.

And yet, the starting point for Améry’s reflections was the experience of exile, expulsion, and torture—and that of being Jewish. As an exiled Jew, he no longer had a homeland. It was irrevocably taken from him, not only in spatial terms, but also as a memory, through the violence he experienced and the silence of neighbors and schoolmates.

Herein lies the difference between the German longing for community, which characterizes the current discourse on *Heimat*, and the *Heimat* nostalgia of yesterday’s and today’s exiles, which would once again do them violence if it is ignored. The homesickness of the displaced refers to the place from which they were expelled; it arises from a longing for the state of affairs before the onset of violence, or simply from a fear for friends and comrades and a desire to be at their side. Memory is supposed to ease the pain of exile and loss. At the same time, it expresses the refusal to let go of the last thing left, to let the oppressors take away the memories as well.

Yearning for a lost homeland conveys the violence that drove people from their homes, and often also of the violence they experience in the shape of discrimination and exclusion in their new place of residence. Things are fundamentally different when the natives proudly profess their love for their homeland; not infrequently, it is even the cause of the others' expulsion. Those who had to flee from the Nazis also had to flee from their idea of *Heimat*, which excluded them and left them to be exterminated. To equate the expellers' love of *Heimat* with the expellees' homesickness is not only cynical, but also creates a false sense of community, a common "we" of victims and perpetrators expressed through the alleged shared love of the homeland.

Many who consider themselves progressives refuse to accept this politically decisive distinction between the homesickness of refugees and the German longing for *Heimat*. In their attempts to justify their love of *Heimat*, they like to invoke Ernst Bloch's utopia of transforming the world into *Heimat* and Kurt Tucholsky's "quiet love" for the German homeland, refusing to see that Bloch was speaking of *Heimat* as a utopia, a non-place in an indeterminate future, and Tucholsky recanted his nationalist gaffes after he, too, was driven out by the Nazi *Heimatschutz*.[18]

Upon closer inspection, it becomes clear that in most cases, a left-wing love of the homeland conceals a reactionary need, namely to whitewash Germans of their historical guilt. And—this must be conceded—it is a desire that did not arise only with the shift to the right. There is a leftist tradition of love of the homeland, and that always means: love of Germany. But this is only possible if the destructive nature of German ideas of community and especially the Nazi era and the Holocaust are not seen as an inseparable part of *Volk* and *Heimat*. Quite a few left-wing fans of *Heimat* offer numerous useful reflections and critical insights on other topics. Unfortunately, they are invoked by those who want to contribute yet another enlightened, progressive version of *Heimat* to current debates.

Yet, it is not enough to criticize a particularly toxic version of community underlying right-wing violence. To be able to counter the violence to come, we need to criticize the concept of *Heimat* itself. This is all the more true in times like ours, when the social climate leaves no doubt as to who is in the majority.

There have been many attempts to give the nation a progressive connotation; they can be traced back to the concept of the *Volksgemeinschaft*. They have neither weakened the Right nor curbed its violence. They have merely caused difficulties for the few who opposed the regressive longing for natural belonging and communitization, cementing their marginal position. And so, adopting the right-wing concept of *Heimat* has not weakened the Right but strengthened it by normalizing its discourse. The simultaneous electoral successes of the FPÖ in Austria and of the AfD in east Germany in September 2024 are impressive proof of this.

The *Heimat* debate is not about how we want to live together, but about who we are, who is allowed to live here, and what customs and rituals they must follow. These are nonnegotiable because they are part of the ground on which we stand, "because we've always done it that way." Every desire for change, every will to emancipation, even critical reflection itself is thus rejected. The

Enlightenment was about thinking for oneself and consciously making decisions, about questioning old worldviews and behaviors rather than submitting to them. Social progress has always consisted in breaking with traditions, this peer pressure from the dead, and rebelling against domination disguised as tradition. *Heimat* demands the opposite; *Heimat* demands submission.

People Are Not Trees

At its core, *Heimat* is a *völkisch* idea because it confuses people with trees. By rooting people in the ground, you incapacitate and subordinate them to nature and the community, turning them into slaves to the smells and tastes of their childhood. The objection, which can be heard and read everywhere, that *Heimat* is just a feeling reinforces the suspicion of its inherent brutality. If only a feeling shared by the majority determines what home is, then the minority oppressed or excluded by it has no authority to appeal to. *Heimat* means tyranny of the majority, "lynch law" and thus "in principle the permission to murder," as Klaus Theweleit put it.[19] *Heimat* cannot tolerate the difference that characterizes every society, and if you want to erase that difference, you have to expel, or at least silence, the people who are responsible for it. *Heimat* is the battle cry with which migrants are chased through the streets and the justification for letting refugees drown in the Mediterranean.

The "right to a homeland"—barring that far-right German expellee associations still understand it as the ethnic claim to the former eastern territories of Germany—inevitably denies that right to others, not least those who don't have the privilege of living in a safe and peaceful place due to wars, climate change, and capitalism. To preserve this privilege for ourselves, others are assigned a natural, customary place, where they are supposed to stay or to which they are to be deported. *Heimat* can only have value in a world in which millions of people are forced to flee. And these people not only fled their homeland, but just as often ran away from a specific idea of it in which they and their relatives had no place. "A homeless person has no home, but an exile believes he has one. However, he has not reckoned with those who have remained in the so-called *Heimat*," Georg Kreisler recalled of his escape from the Nazis.[20] The *Heimat* idyll destroys the memory of its victims. It is not only false but also dangerous. The love of *Heimat* might appear innocent and peaceful, yet it contains hatred for everything that disturbs the supposed idyll.

A progressive answer to the reactionary longing for natural belonging and repressive harmony would be to emphasize difference or becoming human through detachment and contradiction. "Human beings are even more rootless than other animals, and when they do search out their roots, one gets a vegetable impression of them. Truly rooted and settled people . . . are experientially impoverished shrubs."[21] This beautiful sentence comes from philosopher Vilém Flusser, a Czech Jew who escaped the Nazis by fleeing from Prague to London in 1940, from where he moved on to São Paulo, leaving Brazil three decades later due to its military dictatorship. He returned to Europe, living in different places before retiring in a French village. Flusser vividly describes the painful process of flight, exile, and new beginnings in a foreign country as he experienced it firsthand. However, what other people would call uprooting he calls "delivery." Flusser writes that it was only when he was forced to violently cut his cultural and social, supposedly natural bonds that he was first able to choose them freely, to make a conscious decision about them. He speaks of the "freedom won at the expense of heimat" and argues that the migrant experience should be taken as a vision for a cosmopolitan consciousness in the "beckoning future without heimat."[22]

The point is not that everyone should have a *Heimat*, but that no one needs it anymore because the conditions we live in are reasonable and humane at last. *Heimatlosigkeit* is not a defect; it is a cosmopolitan alternative to the intellectual and emotional imprisonment on native soil. It means an end to borders and narrow-mindedness; it is the answer to provincial stuffiness as well as traditional role models and family structures, to the control and self-denial of an oppressive society. *Heimat*, on the other hand, is—as Franz Dobler once so aptly put it—only where you hang yourself.[23]

"Für die Mehrheit der Deutschen ist 'Heimat' positiv besetzt," *Die Welt*, June 12, 2022, https://www.welt.de/politik/deutschland/article239304375/Heimatbegriff-Mehrheit-der-Deutschen-hat-positives-Heimatgefuehl.html.

2 *Bulletin der Bundesregierung* no. 98-1 (October 3, 2017). Unless otherwise noted, all translations are mine.

3 "Özdemir lobt Bundespräsident Steinmeier für Rede zur Einheit," RedaktionsNetzwerk Deutschland, October 4, 2017, https://www.rnd.de/politik/ozdemir-lobt-bundesprasident-steinmeier-fur-rede-zur-einheit-IWKUBAVMCF7AVCEQWZ2YEYNTDU.html.

4 Bodo Ramelow, "Die lasse ich mir von keinem Nazi wegnehmen," interview by Jan Hollitzer and Jonas Schaible, T-Online, March 10, 2018, https://www.t-online.de/nachrichten/deutschland/innenpolitik/id_83367050/bodo-ramelow-laesst-sich-die-heimat-von-keinem-nazi-wegnehmen-.html.

5 Quoted in Johannes Schneider, "Hilfe, es heimatet sehr," *Die Zeit*, October 9, 2017, https://www.zeit.de/gesellschaft/zeitgeschehen/2017-10/heimat-katrin-goering-eckardt-frank-walter-steinmeier.

6 Eike Geisel, *Die Wiedergutwerdung der Deutschen* (Berlin: Edition Tiamat, 2015).

7 "Community" is used here in the sense of the contrast between "society" (*Gesellschaft*) and "community" (*Gemeinschaft*). "Society" refers to the modern form of social interaction of large groups in a common territory, which is characterized by difference, conflict, and negotiation processes and in which belonging and coexistence are based on a "rational agreement by mutual consent." Community, on the other hand, is strongly linked to a collective identity based on a supposedly shared history, origin, traditions, language, and culture. It is always associated with a notion of homogeneity and harmony, and belonging here is based above all on a shared "subjective feeling." See Max Weber, *Economy and Society*, ed. Guenther Roth and Claus Wittich, 2 vols. (Oakland: University of California Press, 1978).

8 Thorsten Mense, "Ein brutales Gefühl," *Neues Deutschland*, December 28, 2018, https://www.nd-aktuell.de/artikel/1108905.debatte-um-heimatbegriff-ein-brutales-gefuehl.html.

9 Christoph Türcke, *Heimat: Eine Rehabilitierung* (Springe: Zu Klampen Verlag, 2006).

10 Sahra Wagenknecht, "Ich bin nicht die geborene Netzwerkerin," interview by Christoph Schwennicke and Christoph Wöhrle, *Cicero*, September 26, 2018, https://www.cicero.de/innenpolitik/sahra-wagenknecht-aufstehen-linke-sammlungsbewegung/plus.

11 Diether Dehm, "Arbeitsteilung statt Spaltung," *Neues Deutschland*, November 14, 2018, https://www.nd-aktuell.de/artikel/1105700.linke-in-der-krise-arbeitsteilung-statt-spaltung.html.

12 KomRex – Zentrum für Rechtsextremismusforschung, Demokratiebildung und gesellschaftliche Integration (Friedrich-Schiller-Universität Jena), *Politische Kultur im Freistaat Thüringen: Heimat Thüringen; Ergebnisse des Thüringen-Monitors 2018*, 121, https://www.komrex.uni-jena.de/komrexmedia/2340/tm-2018-mit-anhang.pdf.

13 Oliver Decker and Elmar Brähler, eds., *Flucht ins Autoritäre: Rechtsextreme Dynamiken in der Mitte der Gesellschaft; Die Leipziger Autoritarismus-Studie 2018* (Gießen: Psychosozial-Verlag, 2018).

14 KomRex, *Politische Kultur im Freistaat Thüringen* (see note 12), 137.
15 Ramelow, "Die lasse ich mir von keinem Nazi wegnehmen" (see note 4).
16 Jean Améry, *Werke*, vol. 7, *Aufsätze zur Politik und Zeitgeschichte*, ed. Irene Heidelberger-Leonard (Stuttgart: Klett-Cotta, 2005), 7.
17 Jean Améry, "Wieviel Heimat braucht der Mensch?" in *Werke*, vol. 2, *Jenseits von Schuld und Sühne / Unmeisterliche Wanderjahre / Örtlichkeiten*, ed. Gerhard Scheit and Irene Heidelberger-Leonard (Stuttgart: Klett-Cotta, 2002), 86–117, here 94.
18 Ernst Bloch, *The Principle of Hope*, trans. Neville Plaice, Stephen Plaice, and Paul Knight (Cambridge, MA: MIT Press, 1986); Kurt Tucholsky, "Heimat," in *Gesammelte Werke*, ed. Mary Gerold-Tucholsky and Fritz J. Raddatz, vol. 7 (Reinbek bei Hamburg: Rowohlt, 1996), 312–14, here 314.
19 Klaus Theweleit at "Heimatphantasien," conference, August 19, 2018, Kampnagel, Hamburg.
20 Georg Kreisler, preface to *Zufällig in San Francisco: Unbeabsichtigte Gedichte* (Berlin: Verbrecher, 2010), 17–18.
21 Vilém Flusser, *The Freedom of the Migrant: Objections to Nationalism*, trans. Kenneth Kronenberg, ed. Anke K. Finger (Champaign: University of Illinois Press, 2013), 25.
22 Ibid., 11, 14.
23 Franz Dobler, *Bierherz: Flüssige Prosa* (Hamburg: Edition Nautilus, 1994), 7.

Anton Jäger

Post-fascism in a Post-democracy

Stuck in American exile in 1941, the German Marxist Karl Korsch surveyed the successes of Hitler's blitzkrieg on Crete and tried, heroically, to offer a socialist interpretation. The German offensive, he wrote in a letter to Bertolt Brecht, expressed "frustrated left-wing energy" and a displaced desire for workers' control.[1] Alexander Kluge and Oskar Negt summarize Korsch's position with reference to the historical background of the German battalions:

> In their civilian life, the majority of the tank crews of the German divisions were car mechanics or engineers (that is, industrial workers with practical experience). Many of them came from the German provinces that had experienced bloody massacres at the hands of the authorities in the Peasant Wars (1524–1526). According to Korsch, they had good reason to avoid direct contact with their superiors. Almost all of them could also vividly remember the positional warfare of 1916, again a result of the actions of their superiors, in whom they had little faith thereafter.... According to Korsch, it thereby became possible for the troops to invent for themselves the blitzkrieg spontaneously, out of historical motives at hand.[2]

It is tempting—and consoling—to view the ascendance of Europe's extreme right in recent years through Korsch's lens. Both new and old provinces conquered by them—from Thuringia to Billancourt, from East Flanders to the Viennese city belt—once counted as socialist fortresses in the 20th century. There, the old demand for workers' control seems to have been perverted into xenophobic passion, a longing to overthrow the bourgeois regime replaced by an attempt to smash its weakest subjects. One wants to believe, with Karl

Korsch, that behind the mask of reaction there is still some potentially emancipatory profile, and that a left-wing edifice can still be rebuilt on the ruin.

A sizeable body of literature in the social sciences built up since the early 1990s—when the far right achieved its first breakthroughs on the continent, from France to the Netherlands—also seems to sanction such a Korschian reading. Together with a growing literature on populism, a "switching thesis" implied that, with the onset of a new, postindustrial society, the European working classes left their abode in communist and socialist parties and migrated to the opposite side of the political spectrum. As Korsch would put it, they deposited their "left-wing energy" elsewhere, in a felicitous convergence of extremes that liberal writers had already detected in the totalitarianisms of the 20th century.

The thesis continued to haunt political discourse throughout the long 1990s. With the far right increasingly taking on a social and even anti-European slant, it attained a plausibility far beyond the confines of the academe alone. It even led some figures to call the new far-right outfits, from the Front national to Jörg Haider's Freedom Party of Austria (FPÖ), workers' parties or nominate them with the title "populist"—a new addition to the social-science vocabulary in the early 1990s. Even if it caught some rhetorical features of the new far right—which had traded an emphasis on racial identity for cultural specificity—this was a term that all too often allowed them to suppress tainted associations with a postfascist tradition and often turned them into freshly appointed stewards of a working class abandoned by its left-wing representatives. At the same time, the term "populist" undoubtedly owed its attraction to the undeniable novelty of some of these parties. With no clear military wings and fascist veterans of yore, they were hard to compare to their progenitors. At the same time, they were clearly driven by the structural decline of party representation across Europe, in which voters left party outfits and joined a newly virtual and undetermined "people," easily seduced by far-right forces, to be remobilized as racist hordes.

The switching thesis was always more than an analytical device, however. Steadily, it mutated into a full-fledged political program, in which left-wing parties were asked to either adjust to and learn from far-right parties *or* scout for a new sociological base altogether, situated in a new middle class and an increasingly diverse urban service proletariat. Since their old electorate had left, a new one had to be found. With terms such as "gaucho-lepénisme" or a "red-brown" politics, this literature thereby not only sanctioned a populist interpretation of the new far right. It also increasingly beckoned the Left to move rightward, following the lead of its own ex-electorate and apostles of concern in the commentariat. Today, the consequence of this switching politics has become even clearer, even as the establishment conservatives still use the idea as an alibi to move further rightward, while parts of the Left seek to regain a lost working-class electorate by applying the tactics used by its new far-right steward, or let go of its peripheral constituency altogether.

There was no shortage of critiques of this switching thesis by the early 1990s. They noted that many of the regions now counted as new right strongholds saw higher rates of abstention than others. They insisted that voters who left communist parties did so out of a disappointment with the market transitions of the 1990s and 2000s—only faintly captured by the notion of "globalization"—and not out of an ineradicable hatred of foreigners.

These critics also insisted that the ties these new voters held with the far right were hardly comparable to the integral social world offered to them by parties on the left, and that their social program lacked any ambition to tackle the growing power of capital. The result was a 21st-century version of what was once called the "ecological fallacy" in fascism studies: the idea that working-class regions that voted fascist suppressed the fact that it was really the middle classes in those regions who voted fascist, not the working classes themselves, who were always an envious absence from fascist party rolls. Rather than a working-class migration to the right, many exurban workers simply dropped out of politics altogether, no longer voting and shedding their member cards. In their regions, sections of their class and the new petty bourgeoisie did make a move to the far right, partly out of fear of labor market competition, partly out of xenophobia, but hardly as a collective entity, with equally radical ambitions. Heinrich Geiselberger has noted how, without "the enemies of socialism," the Right "can only invoke its spectre." With Gáspár Miklós Tamás, Geiselberger prefers to speak of postfascism: an attempt to make citizenship less universal and confine it to national borders, but without the organizational clout that fascists demonstrated in the 20th century. The New Right is therefore "atomised, volatile, swarm-like, with porous borders between gravity and earnestness, sincerity and irony."[3]

Above all, Geiselberger's new politics is consistently informal: the mob that expressed unconditional support for Donald Trump on January 6 does not even have membership lists. QAnon and the anti-lockdown movement are a subculture that thrives mostly on blogs, Instagram, and Facebook groups. There are, of course, prominent QAnon figures—influencers, so to speak. Yet their leadership is not official or mandated by votes. Rather than a militarily drilled mass, we see a roving swarm, incited by a clique of self-selected activists. This informality also manifests itself economically. In the past year, Trump extorted thousands of dollars from his followers and continued to rake in funds without ever building a clear party structure. As early as 1920, sociologist Max Weber noted how charismatic leaders did not pay their followers and backers with fixed salaries, but rather worked through "donations, booty or bequests."[4] Unsurprisingly, charismatic leadership was also a thoroughly unstable mode of rule: succession to the throne could not simply be guaranteed for the mob, which would now have to look for its next redeemer.

The last years have made the switching thesis even more attractive. In eastern Germany, France, Belgium, the United Kingdom, and the Netherlands, proof for a growing working-class vote no longer reducible to simple abstentionists seems undeniable. The interpretative war around this vote has been equally strident. Many insist that the rise of the far right should not be understood as wrongly sublimated left-wing libido, as Korsch had it, but as an expression of late-capitalist rot: not an insurgency to be redirected, but an impulse to be quashed. The essentials of much of this diagnosis are often inarguable: that the class composition of the new far-right voters is not homogeneously proletarian, that they are not responding to events representing any concrete "immigrant threat," that their actions were incited by both the political class and a digital "lumpencommentariat," and that this concatenation owes more to feverish misinformation than to the authentic grievances of the dispossessed. Instead of concerned citizens, it is revanchist lumpen citizens and middle classes who are unable to cope with the fact of social change in the 21st century. A literature on "neofascism" or "late fascism" has sought to place the revenge fantasies of the contemporary far right in this frame, showing how a new setting summons old ghosts.

While the word "populist" is of only limited use when understanding the New Right, "fascist" proves equally constraining. In terms of the favored ideologemes—from "great replacement" to other ethnonationalist fantasies—the continuity with the 20th century is hard to deny. Yet, in politics as in biology, the environment often proves as important as heredity, as historian Christopher Hill once noted, and contemporary fascists must contend with parameters incommensurate with those of their ancestors.[5] These include demilitarization and the absence of a prerevolutionary threat on the left. As Dylan Riley has noted, the peculiarity and the specificity of the far right become clear when contrasted with the fact that fascists were never able to retain any solid working-class support, a point of incessant frustration to many far-right cadres.[6]

Europe's fascists, for one, rose to power in a period of intense social confrontation: Adolf Hitler and Benito Mussolini prevailed after labor movements tried to instigate revolutions and were asked by the elites to stabilize the social order and reestablish labor discipline. A muscular proletariat is conspicuously absent from the European scene today, fatally weakened by deindustrialization and loose labor markets. In contrast to the 1930s, when fascist street violence flourished, the contemporary far right does indeed thrive on demobilization, both electorally and nonelectorally. Giorgia Meloni's party won an election in which nearly four out of ten Italians stayed home, with turnout down by almost 10 percent from the country's previous vote. In France, Marine Le Pen's National Rally (RN) has long received its best tallies in regions that have the highest voter abstention rates—even with recent changes. In Poland, the Kaczyński family behind the Law and Justice party (PiS) rules over a country where fewer than 1 percent of citizens are members of a political party. These are not mass affairs, but rather exercises in orchestrated demobilization and passivity. As David Broder has noted on the Italian case, while the "latest advance for a far-right party in the land of Fascism's birth surely lends itself to evocative analogies," this "does not mean that Mussolini's heirs merely repeat the past in the present, or even that the fascist elements of their culture are always drawn from interwar Italy."[7]

The data indicate the deeply *contemporary* character of Europe's extreme-right surge—the outgrowths of a newly networked radicalism, not a return to *Freikorps* militancy or Boulangist militarism. Hitler and Mussolini promised to forge colonial empires of the kind their French and British competitors had acquired long ago. Their ambition was to break down borders, not to reinforce them. Today's far right, by contrast, seeks to shield the Old World from the rest of the globe, conceding that the continent will no longer be a protagonist in the 21st century, and that the best it can hope for is protection from the postcolonial hordes.

Where does this leave us for an anatomy of today's Right? Keeping in mind these critiques, both the copycats and the denialists face the same problem: while the switching thesis has some empirical support, it proportionally includes more normative commitment than sober scientific analysis. As mentioned, the evidence remains ambiguous and inconclusive. If you look at the Alternative for Germany (AfD) vote, or the Western extreme-right vote in general, what is far more striking is their dependence on demobilization rather than remobilization: working-class voters drop out of politics, some of them migrate to the extreme right, and this small set of defectors is then made to stand in for the entirety of the demobilized class. Demobilization gets mistaken for remobilization, and the Left's strategic conclusion is that politicians should switch just as voters have switched.

Yet the entire premise of this politics can be faulted: working-class voters are experimenting with new parties, but their main response is a mixture of apathy and frustration, not simply rebellious defection. Even those who migrate to the right and generate the optical illusion of a general switch usually have much weaker ties with the new extreme-right parties than they used to have with their previous left outfits. One can clearly see this in northern France, where Le Pen has taken former communist strongholds, and in eastern Germany—once again, the vote for the extreme right is secretive, private, and mainly noncollective, not an explicit engagement, more passive-aggressive than active, more informal than formal. As Didier Eribon stated in his memoir of his former communist parents, his father's migration to the extreme right also had to be expressed in a different register from the communist lifestyle he had adhered to before. "Unlike voting communist, a way of voting that could be assumed forthrightly and asserted publicly," his father's new vote "seems to have been something that needed to be kept secret, even denied in the face of some 'outside' instance of judgment." In contrast to the French Communist Party (PCF), in "voting for the National Front, individuals remain individuals and the opinion they produce is simply the sum of their spontaneous prejudices," an act carried out in the enclosure of the ballot box.[8]

Two poles inherent in the switching thesis can therefore be avoided: presenting the new far right as an authentic expression of working-class grievances, abandoned by an overly progressive left, or depicting it as an exclusively middle-class and elite outfit that only masquerades and simulates its working base, with no proletarian support whatsoever. Similarly, a middle way between economism and culturalism stops short of reducing the far-right surge to a proletarian rebellion or claiming that its voters somehow hallucinate the fact of economic decline. Granted, Europe's extreme-right surge is no twisted expression of "material interests." But this should not lead us into a form of superstructuralism that represses the economic roots of the current crisis; while a Korschian outlook can lapse into lazy apologism, there is also a species of anti-economism that risks obscuring the social terrain and thereby relinquishes the prospect of changing it. To understand the flammable environment at which Europe's pyromaniac far right has taken aim, we need less mass psychology and more political economy.

One neglected aspect is how economic factors underpin the peculiarly schizoid status of immigration in European public life. A cheap supply of labor remained essential following partial deindustrialization in the 1980s and 1990s, as demographic expansion became necessary to sustain the rising service sector and help European industry retain competitiveness on an increasingly hostile world market. Despite all their rhetorical bombast, conservative parties have done little to alter these fragile growth models in the last decades. For instance: the British Conservative Party neither reduced immigration figures over the last decade nor articulated even the mildest equivalent of Bidenist "reshoring," while its base has increasingly been swept up in right-wing ritualism.

Meanwhile, popular dissatisfaction has been rising since at least the late 2000s, with a creeping sense in the lower ends of the labor market that, although it does not cause low wages, immigration remains an indispensable part of the low-wage regime to which the European policy elite is committed. What we have recently witnessed is that discontent's explosion in the "hyperpolitical" form dominating the 2020s: agitation without durable organization, short-lived spontaneism without institutional fortress building. With a new flock of influencers on the far right, these "trigger points," as Steffen Mau, Thomas Lux, and Linus Westheuser have named them, can easily become charged and mobilize voters on the cheap without building a solid party infrastructure.[9]

Today's New Right is an attempt to rhetorically manage and contain this contradiction at the heart of European financialization: an economy dependent on cheap labor for its meager growth rates, unable to deliver meaningful productivity, with a population that increasingly wants the state to mount some kind of systemic intervention.

There is also the international dimension. Is it surprising that nations that style themselves as attack dogs for a declining imperial hegemon, and unconditionally support genocide in the Middle East, would see such belligerence ricochet on the domestic front? The UK, having normalized the ongoing attempt to exterminate a surplus population in Israel and solve the *Palästinenserfrage* (Palestinian question) once and for all, has given a strong impetus to those wishing to enact anti-Muslim violence at home.

Unlike the dominant variants of antisemitism, anti-Islamic sentiment does not usually engage in projections of global omnipotence. It casts the Muslim as a dangerously ambiguous figure. In the zero-sum world of late capitalism, their ability to retain a minimum of communal cohesion is considered to have better equipped them for labor market competition. Rather than a fear of the other, anti-Muslim feeling is a fear of the same: someone in a position of equal dependence on the market, yet thought to be more effective in shielding themselves against its onslaught. At the same time, the Muslim is also seen as a subaltern agent of the abstraction finance has inflicted on the worlds of postwar stability: someone who is out of place, who is causing "borders and boundaries [to] erod[e]," as Richard Seymour puts it.[10]

Among novelists, Michel Houellebecq remains the paragon for this type of far-right argument. Nominally, Houellebecq has often been cast as a fellow traveler of the nationalist international, providing a literary rationale for its "reconquest" of Europe with visions of an impending civilizational collapse. Although he has never called for a vote for Marine Le Pen —he seemed close to doing so in 2013, according to his friend and English translator Gavin Bowd[11]—his novels have always been welcomed in far-right circles. For Alain Finkielkraut—one of the Franco-Jewish intellectuals supposedly forced to vote for Le Pen in the last election for fear of Jean-Luc Mélenchon's Parisian caliphate—Houellebecq has looked for "the truth within things," while the Orbán family invited him to Budapest for a meeting of minds after he claimed that "the wish of the native French population is not that Muslims assimilate, but that they stop robbing and attacking them."[12]

Recent public pronouncements have only further fed skepticism of the writer's views. In an interview discussing French politics, he presaged "a revolt of the people against these elites" but remained disillusioned about the contemporary far right's prospects for power—Jordan Bardella, the Right's millennial celeb, is so "obsessed with the idea of not saying anything that could be perceived badly that he simply says nothing at all," while Marine Le Pen is "neither very intelligent nor very competent." Yet, Houellebecq has also expressed unhappiness with the republican bloc pitted against the party, stating that "the entire elite is mobilizing against the National Front" and that "it would be better if the conflict had broken out now."[13] The same protective ambition becomes visible here. In Jean Raspail's 1973 novel *The Camp of Saints*—a manual for the contemporary far right often seen as an inferior precedent to Houellebecq's own books—the aim is not to conquer Africa but simply to keep its inhabitants south of the Mediterranean.

Houellebecq's oeuvre offers clues beyond our era and about the contemporary far right itself. There is no rival program for government, ethical renaissance, or proper deglobalization. Yet there are rhetorical alternatives to liberalism that electorates are willing to wager on, including growing sections of the Western working class who have lent their votes to parties on the extreme right. Unlike in the 1920s and 1930s, the contemporary far right's success is largely a function of liberalism's failure, not a signal of the Left's strengths—Nazism and fascism, in the end, are only properly conceived as failed revolutions with the actual prerevolutionary situations that preceded them in mind.

Yet, that liberalism has run out of answers in no way implies its rivals are even asking the right questions. The old might indeed be dying, as we are so tirelessly reminded of today. In the case of Houellebecq, however, nothing is even struggling to be born, and the future reeks of stubborn decomposition rather than sudden rebirth. With this, he exemplifies the uneasy successes of the contemporary far right, capturing both its limits and attractions: capable of capitalizing on the failings of a hegemonic liberalism, but hardly able to imagine, let alone enforce, true alternatives to it, just like Honoré de Balzac's clueless monarchists in the 1830s and 1840s. Viewed optimistically, this leaves a space for the Left, which could take the critique of liberalism in a wholly different direction. As Balzac noted in his first published work, a tragedy about Oliver Cromwell, regicide leader of the English Revolution: once a king has lost his head, there is no putting the body back together.

In 1913, Vladimir Lenin controversially claimed that behind the Black Hundreds—the reactionary monarchist force that first gave the world the notion of "pogromism"—one could detect an "ignorant peasant democracy, democracy of the crudest type but also extremely deep-seated." In his view, Russian landowners had tried to "appeal to the most deep-rooted prejudices of the most backward peasant" and "play on his ignorance." Yet "such a game cannot be played without risk," he qualified, and "now and again the voice of the real peasant life, peasant democracy, breaks through all the Black-Hundred mustiness and cliché."[14]

There is no repressed emancipatory core to Europe's extreme-right surge, no "energy" that can be recuperated. In this sense, the kind of desperate hope that Korsch read into the blitzkrieg should be abjured. But underneath the rise of the continental Right still lies a universe of frustration and misery that is the Left's historic task to negate; sometimes, as Lenin noted, the voice of the postindustrial peasant breaks through all the "mustiness and cliché" and speaks as a political agent. Successful strategies for doing so are in short supply and often more palliative than oppositional. A-to-B marches, of the type which now take place in many European cities every month, can be a useful way to assert a political line and remain a minimum requirement of any politics that would stop the far right. But they are inadequate to occupy the void that is now being colonized by Europe's new far right.

1 Quoted in Gunther Martens, “Reclaiming *geballte linke Energie*: War in Alexander Kluge’s Docufiction ‘Heidegger auf der Krim,’” *Seminar: A Journal of Germanic Studies* 50, no. 1 (2014): 69–82, here 75.

2 Alexander Kluge and Oskar Negt, *History and Obstinacy*, ed. Devin Fore, trans. Richard Langston (New York: Zone Books, 2014), 336.

3 Heinrich Geiselberger, “The Attack on the US Capitol Was a Case of ‘Liquid Authoritarianism’ in Action,” *The Guardian*, January 20, 2021, https://www.theguardian.com/commentisfree/2021/jan/20/understand-politics-capitol-breach-authoritarianism-far-right.

4 Max Weber, *Selections in Translation*, ed. W. G. Runciman, trans. Eric Matthews (Cambridge: Cambridge University Press, 1978), 234.

5 Christopher Hill, *The Collected Essays of Christopher Hill*, vol. 2, *Religion and Politics in 17th-Century England* (Brighton: Harvester, 1988), 4.

6 Dylan Riley, foreword to *Fascism and Dictatorship: The Third International and the Problem of Fascism*, by Nicos Poulantzas (London: Verso Books, 2022), ix–xli.

7 David Broder, *Mussolini’s Grandchildren: Fascism in Contemporary Italy* (London: Pluto, 2023), 13.

8 Didier Eribon, *Returning to Reims*, trans. Michael Lucey (Los Angeles: Semiotext(e), 2013), 131, 137.

9 Steffen Mau, Thomas Lux, and Linus Westheuser, *Triggerpunkte: Konsens und Konflikt in der Gegenwartsgesellschaft* (Berlin: Suhrkamp, 2023).

10 Richard Seymour, “Dreaming of Downfall,” *New Left Review*, August 13, 2024, https://newleftreview.org/sidecar/posts/dreaming-of-downfall.

11 Gavin Bowd, *Mémoires d’Outre-France* (Paris: Éditions des Équateurs, 2016), 41.

12 Michel Houellebecq, “Dieu vous entende, Michel,” interview by Michel Onfray, *Front populaire*, November 29, 2022, https://frontpopulaire.fr/articles/dieu-vous-entende-michel_ma_17072512.

13 Michel Houellebecq, “Michel Houellebecq, escritor: ‘Pueden pasar cosas desagradables en Francia,’” interview by Marc Bassets, *El País*, July 6, 2024, https://elpais.com/internacional/2024-07-06/michel-houellebecq-escritor-pueden-pasar-cosas-desagradables-en-francia.html.

14 Lenin, “The Black Hundreds,” in *Collected Works*, vol. 19, *March–December 1913*, ed. Robert Daglish, trans. George Hanna (Moscow: Progress, 1977), 390–91, here 390.

Ingo Niermann

Guilt Su- prem- acy

63

The German engagement with the Nazi past has congealed into a national sense of inherited guilt. Contrary to its anti-racist and anti-totalitarian intentions, this identitarian concept is itself völkisch *and autocratic. Collective narratives of guilt are, in the final analysis, as fascistic as those of collective victimhood. How can historical guilt be individuated?*

A Guiltless Germany

After World War II and the Holocaust ended, guilt was not an issue for the broad majority of Germans. They had remained righteous until the end, regardless of what they had personally done as Nazis or under them. Moreover, the assumption was that the German people as a whole had atoned enough—if atonement was needed at all. The war was lost, Germany's cities lay in ruins, its territories had been ceded, and its partition announced. Over five million soldiers and one million civilians had perished, hundreds of thousands were taken prisoner, and further millions of ethnic Germans were displaced.

After the founding of the Federal Republic of Germany (FRG) in the capitalist West, a series of unanimous parliamentary votes ended and reversed the "denazification" initiated by the Allies. In 1951, the German government pressured them into pardoning most of the Nazis tried and sentenced after the war. Former Nazi civil servants were generously classified as mere "fellow travelers" and had to be rehired. Financial reparations to the Nazis' victims only came later, at first largely limited to German Jews, in addition to one payment to the State of Israel. The restitution of Aryanized Jewish property only commenced haltingly, while the prosecution of those responsible for mass killings dragged on. The Christian churches whitewashed their anti-Judaism by resorting to philosemitic opportunism toward the

Jews as God's chosen people and welcomed their forced return to the Holy Land.

The smaller German Democratic Republic (GDR), on the other hand, was ruled by the Socialist Unity Party (SED), much of whose leadership had ostensibly faced Nazi persecution. The GDR thus cast itself as a nation of victims while vilifying the FRG as a nation of perpetrators. This appeared as little more than cheap propaganda to FRG citizens. The "economic miracle" of West Germany's rapid recovery proved that they had drawn the longer straw—both economically and in terms of civil rights—by aligning themselves with the capitalist West. Their part of Germany would rise from the ruins richer than ever.

West Germans were so at peace with themselves that the number of members of the Bundestag who had been members of the Nazi Party increased from election to election. It peaked in 1965 at around 25 percent, twenty years after the end of the Third Reich and in parallel to the first federal case against concentration camp personnel (the so-called Frankfurt Auschwitz trials). Most of these ex-Nazis belonged to the parties of the ruling coalition, the Christian Democrats (CDU/CSU) and the Liberals (FDP).

The horror of the Nazi atrocities only reached a broader West German public when a new generation came of age in Western Europe. The so-called sixty-eighters questioned the anti-communist common sense of the postwar era, and, in 1969, Social Democrat Willy Brandt was elected chancellor. He had spent the Nazi years in exile, for which his political opponents defamed him as a traitor.

Did the retroactive outrage over the Third Reich have consequences at the later time? Sure, financial reparations could be made, and old Nazi thugs could be hunted down and brought behind bars. But for many sixty-eighters, these were reactionary pedantries. After all, they were already fighting for a society free of oppression in which everybody would care for everybody, educating and forgiving one another instead of judging and incarcerating. The best way of atoning for Nazi atrocities would be to build such a liberated society.

This approach was ideologically underpinned by the Frankfurt School, founded in the 1920s by Marxists, mostly of Jewish origin, some of whom returned from exile. According to them, every late capitalist society had fascist tendencies. The Holocaust was the final stage of capitalist exploitation (even corpses were put to use), and as long as capitalism remained in place, the danger of a new Holocaust—against Jews or other marginalized groups—would not be overcome.

In the FRG, this line of argument sounded all the more plausible as many of its business and political leaders had been active in the Third Reich. What appeared as opportunistic adaptability or perhaps even humanistic responsiveness immediately after the war was now taken as proof that capitalism and fascism were essentially the same. This lent particular fervor to the West German student movement and, at the same time, served to exonerate any specific family guilt. If Nazism was the final stage of capitalism, then, according to the Marxist understanding of history as a dialectical unfolding of contradictions, it was ultimately an inevitable stage of social development. Thus, the communist struggle of the sixty-eighters developed a particular radicalism in West Germany. Several terrorist organizations sprang up and enjoyed widespread support, as did postcolonial liberation movements and the struggle of the displaced and oppressed Palestinians against Israel.

The Nationalism of Guilt

It did not take long for the dream of a great leftist revolution to dissipate yet again. The more moderate sixty-eighters followed student protest leader Rudi Dutschke's call for a "long march through the institutions," bringing along a new awareness of Nazi atrocities.

The sixty-eighters had, in Biblical terms, failed in their attempt at an earthly return to paradise. Fascism always persisted in a more or less latent form along with capitalism—finding its most horrific expression in the German people. They would still bear the stain of Nazi crimes even if the last old Nazi had died and all citizens had the "blessing of a late birth" that Chancellor Helmut Kohl claimed for himself during his first state visit to Israel in 1984, meaning that he and his contemporaries could not possibly have participated in the Nazi regime.

Just as Christians inherit original sin from Adam and Eve, Germans would now inherit the guilt of Nazism. After eating from the tree of knowledge, Adam and Eve realized that they were naked and grew ashamed, only thus becoming civilized human beings. The Germans, on the contrary, had shamelessly proven that even a *Kulturnation* (nation of culture) could lay itself bare, displaying a beastliness wilder than the beasts.

There was some comfort in believing that the German people would always be special. The 20th century had seen several genocides with millions killed, but none had been as perfectly organized as the Holocaust, none were perpetrated by a nation as technically and intellectually advanced as Germany, and none had been committed against the Biblical "chosen people." While Germany had produced famous "poets and thinkers" in the 18th and 19th centuries to catch up in a civilizational race, it had then produced the greatest imaginable horror (as far as it was imaginable at all). Only by becoming aware of itself as an archetype of evil did the German nation perfect itself in the sense of the dialectical philosophy of history developed by Georg Wilhelm Friedrich Hegel.

The more Germans came to enjoy "the blessing of a late birth," the more they took a liking to this "pride in their sins," as philosopher Hermann Lübbe put it.[1] The inveterate who just wanted to be proud of their fatherland like members of other nations were outraged by a "national masochism" and "cult of guilt." But most West Germans were happy to go along with it as their country reaped praise for openly confronting the darkest chapter of German, indeed, human history. Year after year, its dignitaries repeated on several days of remembrance how uniquely horrific Nazism had been and how important it was that it never return.

Words alone, however, were not enough: action had to follow. For the sixty-eighters, action had still been directed against the persisting sociopolitical order; now, a special moral obligation was delegated to the state, while the few remaining or returning Jews were allotted the role of perpetual victims. This outsourcing of guilt and conscience, in turn, implied that all appeals for "civic engagement" would ultimately mean that citizens were expected to be loyal to the reformed, morally obligated state.

As for the FRG's special responsibilities arising from its hereditary guilt, this was a subject that could have been bitterly contested, as it occasionally was. However, a state that is constantly trying to prove its goodness has to strive for something that not only brings lasting benefits to others but also to itself. This was to be the particularly zealous pursuit of European unification, something all established Western German parties agreed upon.

- First, European identity served as a substitute for simple, blameless nationalism. Europe was not Aryan, but at least it was White. Viewed as a whole, Europe had been far more felonious than Germany on its own, but, except for the Crusades, it had never been so as a unified force. European unification was seen as a project rooted in Christian values, but the Crusades had taken place more than five hundred years ago, while the missionary coercion of the colonial era had been embedded in the nation-states. The United States was left to do the dirty imperialist work of the Cold War: overthrowing left-wing governments and supporting right-wing dictatorships.

- Second, a Europe largely freed of trade barriers offered Germany the opportunity to compete economically with its wartime enemies. Germany gave patronizing support to the community's new member states, providing subsidies to dominate them economically time and again. The more countries joined European integration, the greater Germany's economic triumph. Unlike a military victory, this triumph was a win-win situation, as it spurred Western Europe as a whole on to greater achievements, thus strengthening general prosperity.

All in all, the FRG liked to see itself in the trinity of a new civil religion: guilt nationalism was the Father, Europeanism the Holy Ghost, and generous economic triumphalism their corporeal Son. Depending on context and personal preference, you could focus on one of them, but you were basically honoring all three.

Reunification as a Crisis of Identity

Just over four decades after the end of the Third Reich, something happened that few would have thought possible so soon, despite all the lip service paid to the cause: the Iron Curtain fell, and reunification was within reach. As GDR citizens were at an economic disadvantage, reunification also had its charitable side. It was thus the GDR that joined the FRG in 1990. Nevertheless, the identitarian trinity of the FRG was seriously shaken:

— The obsolete East German industry collapsed, and despite huge subsidies and investments into ailing infrastructure, unemployment skyrocketed. Germany was drawn into a fiscal downward spiral and became the "sick man of Europe."

— The dissolution of the Eastern Bloc not only reunited Germany but also the economies of Eastern and Western Europe. This meant not only larger markets but also cheaper labor and outsourcing opportunities. The economically marginalized East Germans saw little reason to embrace European unification and preferred traditional xenophobic nationalism.

— Likewise, West German guilt nationalism was not well received in the East, since the GDR was supposedly the nation of those who had suffered under the Nazis. At the same time, West Germans felt obliged to make a special gesture of contrite humility in response to the "gift" of reunification. When the Berlin Holocaust Memorial was proposed, it divided Germany. For some, it was a paragon of national shame; for others, the memorial itself was shameful. Attacks on Jewish institutions became more frequent.

Nevertheless, reunited Germany would continue to insist upon its identitarian trinity. After all, the collapse of the Eastern Bloc was followed by a rapid advance in European integration. In 1993, the European Community became the European Union (EU), and it seemed foreseeable that it would span the entire continent, except Russia and a few outliers. The German economy stuttered, but reunification eventually made it larger and more important. And guilt nationalism caught on. Other Western countries also began to acknowledge their guilt for historical atrocities such as colonialism, slavery, genocide, and the oppression of Indigenous peoples. Germany no longer appeared as the one evil, out-of-control Western nation, but only as one where things had gone particularly badly and that, in turn, had also been quickest to start dealing with the past. All in all, Germany had turned into a more normal nation, yet it was still an extraordinary one.

While Germany stayed the course and slowly picked itself up economically, the Western world was beset by a series of devastating crises. Initially, Germany felt vindicated: after 9/11, it held back from supporting the US, also with reference to the Nazi past, "only" deployed troops to already occupied parts of Afghanistan, and did not invade Iraq. As for the 2009 global financial crisis and the subsequent euro debt crisis, Germany emerged relatively unscathed; after the country's costly reunification, it had kept a relatively tight rein on its budget and avoided creating any economic bubbles.

The identitarian trinity of guilt nationalism, Europeanism, and economic triumphalism had been consolidated; only, the world was no longer the same. While Europe faced ever-greater economic competition from China, India, and other Southeast Asian countries, Africa and the Arab world presented a demographic challenge with millions of young people willing to migrate. As for Russia, it challenged Europe's security policy with an army financed by billions in natural-resource revenues.

The EU was unprepared for these challenges. It ignored the growing strength of non-Western powers and was caught cold on three fronts (the refugee crisis since 2015, the Russo-Ukrainian war and the accompanying energy crisis since 2022, and, running parallel to both, a steadily intensifying cold war with China). Yet again, the identitarian trinity risked being supplanted by the kind of traditional, xenophobic nationalism that had been rampant in other European countries for a while.

Angela Merkel's Israel Doctrine

During this period of mounting international crises, 2005 to 2021, Germany was ruled by Angela Merkel in various coalitions. Her party, the Christian Democratic Union (CDU), had also provided the first federal chancellor, Konrad Adenauer, but like all parties represented in the German parliament, it now propagated the identitarian trinity—that is, until the aforementioned crises fueled the rise of the nationalist, far-right Alternative for Germany (AfD).

The East German Merkel was popular because of her pragmatism in responding to the crises acutely affecting Germany, Europe, and the Western world- and in promptly sweeping them under the carpet again. Before reunification, Merkel had been adept at making a name for herself in youth and trade union work, despite her skeptical view of the GDR's Socialist regime. She now put this skill to good use in international negotiations and party work.

Fundamentally conservative, Merkel knew how to rapidly change tack whenever she saw she had no other option. As a physicist, she had initially been a strong supporter of nuclear energy, but after the 2011 Fukushima nuclear disaster, she advocated phasing out nuclear power and increased dependence on Russian gas. While she, like most East Germans, had at first been skeptical of a multicultural society ("multiculturalism has failed"),[2] she advocated a charitable, integrative "welcome culture" when hundreds of thousands of refugees arrived in Germany in 2015.

With every about-face, a growing number of Germans saw Merkel as a traitor to conservative values. Some even insinuated that she was a Trojan horse sent by the defunct GDR. No matter how motherly and level-headed Merkel appeared to most people in view of her tactical skill—reminiscent of the first German chancellor, Otto von Bismarck—in the end, her actions only served to confirm the crisis in Europe. Europeanism was becoming less and less useful for the identitarian trinity.

In its place, Merkel recast Germany's particular historical responsibility as unconditional loyalty to Israel and its government, regardless of its ethnonationalism. During her time in office, Merkel, the daughter of a Protestant pastor, traveled to Israel seven times, declaring, to great applause, Israel's security to be Germany's unconditional "reason of state."

Before, the only political movement to have done so resolutely were the so-called anti-Germans, a splinter group of the extreme left formed after reunification. They were driven by the fear of a new German quest for hegemony, a quest that an anti-Western left would also encourage. This fear had evaporated. Now, swearing allegiance to Israel was an easy way to feed the German superiority complex.

— Recently, German acknowledgment of historical guilt had become more and more inclusive, as not only Jews but also Sinti and

Roma, disabled people, and homosexuals had been exterminated in the concentration camps. And then, there were the crimes against international law already committed during the colonial era. The legacy of guilt had grown, yet at the same time, it appeared less special, now that other Western countries had also begun critically reviewing their histories. It was only by focusing on the systematic extermination of God's chosen people that Germany could continue to cast itself as a "nation of culture" unparalleled in its fall and resurrection.

— Once the European economic ascent stalled, Germany's role as its motor was in question. At this point, reparations claims from states once occupied and oppressed by the Third Reich piled up. In contrast, both the Central Council of Jews in Germany and the State of Israel had stopped making substantial material claims. Significant reparation payments had already been made, the number of Jews in Germany was negligible, and the number of living Holocaust survivors dwindled year by year. Guaranteeing the State of Israel's existence came cheap, given that the US was already providing its tangible military and geopolitical support, propelled by an unholy alliance of predominantly liberal Jews and fundamentalist Christians who honor Israel as biblical prophecy.

— The Israeli government and its supporting organizations equated virtually all criticism of the State of Israel with antisemitism (in line with the examples of antisemitism given by the International Holocaust Remembrance Alliance), thereby creating an all-purpose political weapon not only against right-wing extremists but also against leftists and Muslim immigrants. Solidarity with the Palestinians oppressed by Israel is deemed to be just as antisemitic as criticism of the "globalist" agenda of Jewish billionaires. Conspiracy theories are considered antisemitic per se, as they are reminiscent of *The Protocols of the Elders of Zion*. Thus, anyone who deviates from the officially determined opinion corridor can easily be dismissed as an antisemite.

But just like the cheap Russian gas Merkel had placed her hopes in—instead of promoting renewable energy—the Zionist definition of antisemitism came at a devastating price:

— Despite the absence of any imminent danger, severe and arbitrary restrictions were placed on freedom of speech. With each new major crisis, such as the mass influx of refugees, climate change, the COVID-19 pandemic, the Russian invasion of Ukraine, the Hamas attack on Israel, and the subsequent invasion of Gaza, it was initially possible to mobilize significant segments of the population to express solidarity or provide humanitarian aid. Meanwhile, any member of the public who voiced doubts about the way a crisis was presented by the established parties and media was in danger of being branded an antisemite.

— Unconditional loyalty to the increasingly radical ethnonationalist Israeli government effectively made a mockery of all warnings about the rise of right-wing extremism in Germany. The claim of erecting a "firewall" against the AfD quickly became implausible; as a last resort, the party would have to be accused of planning a coup to seek its prohibition or declare a state of emergency.

— With the fall of the Iron Curtain, Berlin had become a center of the international cultural world. However, the only relevant multicultural structure in Germany faced the threat of an abrupt demise when, after the Hamas attack, there were renewed calls for loyalty to the Israeli military, no matter how oppressive its occupation or how brutal its vengeance. Even calls for a ceasefire were condemned as antisemitic. The German cultural world was in danger of being provincialized well before any nationalist takeover.

Anti-Identitarian Identitarianism

Nowadays, self-victimization dominates political discourse. This is often blamed on the identity politics of marginalized groups. Instead of rising as a united, oppressed class, each group tries to individually evoke outrage over their respective plight.

But the urge to see ourselves primarily as victims has its origins in bourgeois humanism. Humanism fosters a sense of personal responsibility, but such responsibility is contingent on certain fundamental freedoms. Once these are restricted, the individual becomes a victim whose grievances cry for redress. The more fully one seeks to safeguard these freedoms, the greater the number of actions that will be perceived as impinging upon the freedoms of others. Therefore, being an agent is an ever more delicate matter, requiring comprehensive safeguards and assurances. If push comes to shove, it is better to convincingly play the part of a victim.

In their manic hero worship, the Nazis also cast themselves first and foremost as victims—whether of a Jewish world conspiracy, the Treaty of Versailles, or a fictitious Polish war of aggression. Accordingly, World War II and the Holocaust served the cause of acute or preventive self-defense. It was therefore easy for the Nazis to see themselves as victims even after the Third Reich had fallen.

All identity politics is fascistic in that it collectivizes certain narratives of victimhood and prioritizes them over others. The only difference is that, in its critical form, it does so with the paradoxical demand of a general questioning of collective self-prioritization—it draws its authority precisely from that which it seeks to overcome.

The concept of German hereditary guilt inverts this tactical fascism. While critical identity politics externalizes its object of critique (for example, claiming Black identity to contest the discriminatory attribution of blackness), hereditary guilt turns identity politics against itself: one asserts a community of descent by condemning its assertion as the cause of Nazism. Guilt is to blame for the persistence of the identitarian category of the *Volk*.

The only way of resolving this paradox is, as mentioned above, a dialectical one. To do so collectively would require some form of totalitarian synchronization. Instead, the country is being divided into well-meaning Germans and incorrigible ones. Initially, those who showed the goodwill to acknowledge hereditary guilt distinguished themselves from those who stubbornly refused to do so and were often burdened with personal guilt. By now, however, practically every political group among indigenous Germans knows how to use the concept of hereditary guilt for its own purposes. This excludes postwar immigrants and their descendants. The German culture of remembrance discredits Muslim immigrants in particular; as Esra Özyürek explains, they can at best attach themselves to the German sense of hereditary guilt as "subcontractors" and at worst presume to identify with the Jewish victims.[3] To overcome German national guilt supremacy, anyone who feels connected to Germany in any way would have to confront its historical guilt on an individual basis.

Perpetrators Anonymous

The German doctrine of hereditary guilt can be dated to 1970, when Chancellor Willy Brandt fell to his knees at the Warsaw Monument to the Ghetto Heroes to honor the Jewish victims of Nazism. The Nazis had killed by far the largest number of Jews in Poland: over three million. Most of their death camps were also located there. Brandt's genuflection was inconvenient for the antisemitic Polish government. A majority of West Germans also condemned it as an exaggerated gesture of humility—especially since Brandt himself had no part in the crimes of Nazism. It seemed as if he were asking for forgiveness on behalf of the Germans, just as Jesus had asked God for forgiveness on behalf of humanity.

But the chancellor himself did not want his kneeling to be seen in this way. Some thirty years later, he explained in his memoirs: "From the bottom of the abyss of German history, under the burden of millions of victims of murder, I did what human beings do when speech fails them."[4] When he knelt, he saw himself primarily as a human being and not as a part or representative of the German people—not as someone asking for absolution but as someone kneeling in a gesture of humility. The symbolism of this act was so powerful precisely because it was perceived as an expression of deep personal upheaval.

Such tumultuous, epochal moments cannot be repeated or surpassed. The more German hereditary guilt became established as a state concept, the more its expression became a cliché. The concept of hereditary guilt was so successful because it helped to mask the horror of Nazism with well-rehearsed commemoration and mourning formats.

In Germany, school visits to a concentration camp are to this day only compulsory in a handful of federal states. No more than 55 percent of adults have ever visited a camp, and many students are reluctant to undergo the ordeal. What is missing from the civil-religious concept of hereditary guilt are poignant rituals that can be adapted to the needs of the individual.

Comprehensively engaging with the Nazi regime can trigger a range of emotions: horror, anger, shame, sadness, and possibly even fascination and enthusiasm. These can in turn lead to very different feelings of guilt: the guilt of descent, of acquiescence, of indifference, of repression. It is up to you whether you want to entertain these feelings of guilt in the future, whether you want to make amends or repent. Thought is not (yet) subject to prohibitions. For those who feel alone with their possibly forbidden or merely overwhelming thoughts, Perpetrators Anonymous meetings might be a solution, as they would provide a safe space to share feelings of guilt.

When organizing such gatherings, it is crucial to make sure there are always experienced members present, in addition to novices and infrequent attendees. They ought to have a modicum of psychological experience and confer regularly. These experienced members offer personalized guidance to novices and talk to them about how to give their feelings of guilt the necessary space in their lives, how to ensure that they do not get out of hand, and how to alleviate them through acts of kindness.

Perpetrators Anonymous condemns self-flagellation as conceited. Suicides are, in principle, accepted as penance, though those who express such intentions are encouraged

to first share with people outside Perpetrators Anonymous and with euthanasia organizations.

If Perpetrators Anonymous catches on, it will probably lead to similar groups emerging for other forms of unpunishable guilt: the guilt of having or not having had an abortion; the guilt of belonging to a particular race or hating it, of belonging to a particular class or hating it, or of belonging to a particular gender or hating it; the guilt of having too many or no children; the guilt of not showing others enough affection or of oppressing them with one's love; the guilt of having directly or indirectly harmed or killed nonhuman life or of intending to do so in the future; the guilt of having directly or indirectly killed or injured human life or of intending to do so, for example on the road or through one's diet.

The feelings of guilt of the various Perpetrators Anonymous groups could be diametrical opposites, and they could also diverge greatly within a group. The multitude of guilt complexes puts into perspective hereditary guilt related to the Holocaust and the Third Reich—eighty years after their end—but also puts it beyond the reach of paternalistic expropriation by the state and civil institutions. Perpetrators Anonymous would help us to generally admit our mistakes more readily and see ourselves more as agents than victims.

1 Quoted in Henryk M. Broder, “Im Chor der Gutmenschen,” *Der Spiegel*, September 24, 1995, 34. Unless otherwise noted, all translations are mine.

2 Sabine Siebold, “Merkel Says German Multiculturalism Has Failed,” Reuters, October 17, 2010, https://www.reuters.com/article/world/merkel-says-german-multiculturalism-has-failed-idUSTRE69F1K3/.

3 Esra Özyürek, *Subcontractors of Guilt: Holocaust Memory and Muslim Belonging in Postwar Germany* (Stanford, CA: Stanford University Press, 2023).

4 Willy Brandt, *My Life in Politics*, trans. Anthea Bell (London: Hamish Hamilton, 1992), 200.

Boris Buden

Imagined Communities: The Horror of an Afterlife

1

The best vantage point from which to start rereading Benedict Anderson's famous *Imagined Communities* today is the author's extraordinary intellectual sincerity. In the afterword to the 2006 edition of his classic, Anderson comments on the huge success of the book, which has been published in thirty-three countries and twenty-nine languages. "This spread," he writes, "has much less to do with its qualities than its original publication in London, in the English language," which he compares to "a kind of global-hegemonic, post-clerical Latin."[1] If the book had originally been published elsewhere, in a language other than English—Anderson gives examples: in Tirana, in Albanian, or even in Melbourne, in "Australian"—it would obviously not have traveled that far (*IC*, 207).

For Anderson, the global success of his book clearly has much more to do with the conditions of its production, the language in which it is written, and the geopolitical and cultural location of its publisher than with its content, the ideas and arguments it expresses. He is, moreover, fully aware of finally having lost ownership of his text. The afterword—tellingly titled "Travel and Traffic: On the Geo-Biography of *Imagined Communities*"—concludes with the sentence: "*Imagined Communities* is not my book any more" (*IC*, 229). This is not just another self-deconstruction of authorship. Openly mocking "the ludicrous American insistence on 'intellectual' (!) property rights" (*IC*, 229), Anderson willingly sacrifices ownership of the book for the benefit of its expropriators: his translators and publishers. The afterword tells the story of how the book was translated throughout the world, who initiated these translations and why, who the translators were, how he collaborated with them, or how his attempts to do so failed. It discusses publishers' varying interests and motives. While the German edition of 1988 was motivated simply by book reviews in the UK "quality press," the Yugoslav one of 1990 hoped that it might help prevent the country's bloody self-destruction. Translations were also propelled by other factors, some of which, such as purely commercial ones, didn't have anything to do with the book's ideas. Some translations, according to Anderson, even improved the original: "The French version contained elegancies of which I had not dreamed with reorderings which allowed me to see what I 'really' meant, but could not properly express" (*IC*, 229).

The translational travelogue of *Imagined Communities* is much more than an appendix—a delayed afterword—to the book's content. It is a testimony to the openness of its meaning in the contingency of history and the endless diversity of the world, a "continued life" of Anderson's English original, which is how Walter Benjamin understood translation.[2] With the translational postscript, Anderson pointed to the very core of his research into nation and nationalism: the problem of language. And he did so from the perspective of an allegedly marginal linguistic practice, moving it into the focus of our understanding of the world and its history.

It is from this standpoint, that is, from the concrete historical experience of language-in-translation, that today's understanding of *Imagined Communities* should depart. Anderson diagnoses our historical moment precisely on the ground of this experience, looking back on his book's translational world tour: "[T]his proliferation of translations suggests that the force of vernacularization, which, in alliance with print-capitalism, eventually destroyed the hegemony of Church Latin and was midwife to the birth of nationalism, remains strong half a millennium later" (*IC*, 208). But what is actually meant by this "vernacularization"? Where does its force—still, after hundreds of years—come from?

And how does it keep nationalism so fresh and alive—if at all?

2

One can hardly overestimate the importance of "vernacularization" in Anderson's theory of nation and nationalism. What he calls "imagined communities" are in fact "*vernacularly* imagined communities" (*IC*, 79; emphasis mine). The imagination he has in mind was made possible by the vernacular turn, the replacement of the old sacred languages—Latin, Greek, Hebrew, and Church Slavonic—by various vernaculars spoken among the population of premodern Europe, the historical process that elevated them from the everyday linguistic praxis of plebeian crowds to the new print-languages of emerging nations. It is only in these new print-languages that the abstraction necessary for nation formation could eventually be realized as the ability of individuals to "visualize in a general way the existence of thousands and thousands like themselves" (*IC*, 77). This imagined commonality enabled the bourgeoisie to gather around itself a population that we call "nation" today.

The problem, however, lies in the very concept of "vernacularization." While it pretends to have identified and clarified the historical process—in terms of a sociolinguistic transformation—that decisively facilitated the creation of modern nations, it seems, at the same time, to have concealed and obscured similar or even contradictory transformative processes playing an equally important role in the genealogy of modern nation formation and our understanding of this phenomenon. In his theory of nation and nationalism, Anderson's "vernacularization" looks rather heuristically overcharged and, even more obviously, historically overstretched. Is it really true that this transformative process hasn't itself been subjected to transformation—for almost half a millennium?

If "vernacularization" originally meant the creation of print-languages out of spoken vernaculars in early modern Europe, in 15th-century Germany or Italy, does it still mean the same in the world of global capitalism at the turn of the 21st century, under the conditions of rapidly spreading digitalization? How, if at all, has it managed to preserve its force despite all the political, cultural, and technological transformations our languages have undergone through all these centuries?

One can also judge books by what they don't talk about. *Imagined Communities* is marked by the curious absence of a concept. The historical process of the so-called standardization of languages is not mentioned anywhere. Anderson does speak of "the print elevation of languages" (*IC*, 80), which he understands in terms of the publication of grammars and dictionaries serving to standardize "literary [that is, print-]language" (*IC*, 74). He mentions, for instance, the case of the Russian Academy, which at the end of the 18th and the beginning of the 19th century produced a Russian dictionary and an official grammar. Yet he still conceives this standardization as implied in the process of vernacularization, concretely as "a triumph of the vernacular over Church Slavonic" (*IC*, 73). The fact that it is, at the same time, a triumph of the new standard language over the vernacular is of no interest to Anderson. His conflation of vernacularization with standardization to the detriment—suppression—of the latter has far-reaching consequences for his understanding of nation and nationalism. It has made him blind to an antagonism constitutive of the process of vernacularization and, more generally, of the very concept of national (print-, or standard) language. In addition, it has rendered him unable to recognize the radical transformations the national language went through from the time of its standardization until today. In other words, ignoring standardization has prevented Anderson from critically historicizing language and its role in contemporary nation formation.

But what is this antagonism about? I already mentioned it: it is the antagonism between the new standard language and the vernaculars, first the one the standard subjected to its norms and rules and then the others not lucky enough to provide the base for the standard, which were either degraded to the status of dialects or simply eradicated. The birth of the so-called standard language resembles hatching a cuckoo in the vernacular nest that then claims all the nation's care at the expense of other vernaculars, pushing some of them to death. Standardization is known to have an enormous destructive potential. It is "a process of devouring networked speech collectives (the biting of the parts of speech networks in the transformation of the ethnic groups into nations, 'the people's languages' into 'national ones') in order to chew not only their words and sentences but also the palate, the larynx, the lungs, the belly with which they were uttered."[3]

Why doesn't Anderson problematize this? Why does he erase standardization from the historical experience of the sociolinguistic transformation he calls "vernacularization," which he praises for its emancipatory character without accounting for its deep contradictions?

3

Anderson's theory of nation and nationalism, which is at the same time a theory of language as the constitutive element of nation formation, is fundamentally influenced by the historical event that defined the modern age, the bourgeois revolution of the 18th and 19th centuries, and by the ideology that conceptualized its values, the Enlightenment. The emancipatory charge released by this event permeates Anderson's entire theoretical construct, especially his concept of vernacularization. His theory of nation and nationalism is essentially a sociolinguistic allegory of the bourgeois revolution. Like the revolutionary heroes of the Third Estate, the vernaculars of the plebeian masses rose against the ancien régime of the old sacred languages to form the republic of standard national languages, the new international order, the world of nation-states and their languages-of-state. And it is this same world through which *Imagined Communities* has been traveling since its first publication, from translation to translation, from nation to nation, from one to another national culture, from one to another—however diverse, always comparable and commensurable—economic and political condition. The force of vernacularization, which Anderson praises and finds strong even at the outset of the 21st century, is the still-sounding echo of bourgeois emancipation.

But his theory is also one of the international world order that emerged out of the ruins of World War I, under which the old dynastic empires of the Habsburgs, Hohenzollerns, Romanovs, and Ottomans were buried. This historical process was finally concluded after World War II, more precisely by the mid-1970s, when the Portuguese Empire had vanished from the map of the modern world. Not only did the nation now become an international norm; it established, as its constitutive element, a new global order based on normative standards and, consequently, on the system of international law. As "popular, vernacular-based nationalisms" spread from Europe to the entire world (*IC*, 137), they were also absorbed into the consciousness of a new international society. At the same time, the marriage of nationalism to internationalism became, Anderson argues, "undivorcible" (*IC*, 207). This marriage, that is, 21st-century internationalism, is what he believes to have finally replaced the universalism of the old empires.

To understand Anderson's picture of the world as a cluster of nations, their nation-states, and the political relations among them, from which the international order is made, one must again turn to the central category of *Imagined Communities*: language. To claim its importance for his theory of nation and nationalism, the author refers to Hugh Seton-Watson's thesis that such a theory should bring together conventional political, economic, and social history with the history of language.[4] For Anderson, the attention Seton-Watson paid to language in his *Nations and States* is clearly the "most valuable aspect" of this book (*IC*, 71). *Imagined Communities* fully applies his thesis. The rise of nations and nationalist movements and the establishment of modern nation-states and the international order are explained by bringing together a historical event, the bourgeois revolution, and its sociolinguistic equivalent, the "philological-lexicographic revolution," as Anderson calls it (*IC*, 83)—meaning, without mentioning it explicitly, the standardization of the vernaculars, the production of grammars and mono- and bilingual dictionaries. If the bourgeois revolution postulated the equality of all citizens of the republic, the philological-lexicographic revolution created a relation between languages in which they could all meet on equal footing, a relation rendered possible by bilingual dictionaries. As the main tool of the rising industry of translations, they, according to Anderson, "made visible" an egalitarianism among languages: "Whatever the political realities outside, within the covers of the Czech-German/German-Czech dictionary the paired languages had a common status" (*IC*, 71).

Is he right? Have bilingual dictionaries really "made visible" the equality of languages, or have they rather created an illusion of it? Anderson did not ask himself this. We, however, have good reason to do so. Are Slovenian and English, for instance, really equal today? If we encounter them in a bilingual dictionary, it seems that for each word in the one, there is an equivalent in the other. One is inclined to believe that whatever one can say in one of these two languages, one can also say in the other. But why then is much of Slovenian philosophy now originally written in English, while there is no British or American contemporary philosophy originally written in Slovenian? There are around two million Slovenian speakers. English speakers, both those considered "native" and those for whom it is a so-called second language, are counted in the hundreds of millions, including very many Slovenians. Why is this obvious inequality no topic for Anderson?

The conflation of political and linguistic transformation, of the bourgeois and the "philological-lexicographic" revolution, has its price. Anderson's revolutionary vernacular, a nation's standard language, is Janus-faced. It resembles the citizen of a republican nation-state divided into two different figures: the *bourgeois* as an egoistic individual of flesh and blood who pursues his or her private interests and grabs power and wealth to climb the scale of social hierarchy, and the *citoyen*, who is equal in their rights and duties to all other citizens and willingly obeys the law and order of the state that applies equally to all. In his grand narrative, Anderson follows only the history of the "language-*citoyen*," a standardized vernacular around which the national community gathers and in which it imagines itself, the history that leads straight to the existing international order, the world of nations and their languages, all different but equal, a world in which the marriage of nationalism to internationalism, however unhappy, can never be dissolved, as though it were blessed by a god and not entered into by humans.

4

If Anderson had chosen to follow another history of nations and nationalisms, that of the "language-*bourgeois*," he would have arrived at a fundamentally different conclusion about the contemporary "international order." Let's try it ourselves, at least at a few critical points.

4.1

As stated above, Anderson sees the sociolinguistic process of "vernacularization" only from its positive, emancipatory side, ignoring its deeply contradictory character, which is why he could project its linear historical development into the 21st century. However, the actual reality has turned out very differently. Today, one can understand vernacularization as a historically reversible process. "Revernacularization" refers to a linguistic, cultural, and social regression: concretely, the deterioration of a standard national language to the status of a former vernacular. This is, of course, the consequence of the rise of English as a global lingua franca. In our age, English not only dominates an abstract global space above the national languages but has started to increasingly suppress these within the realms of their own cultures, economies, and political and educational institutions. It pushes them out of all the higher discourses of the material, social, and intellectual reproduction of national life and relegates them to the vernacular domains of everyday life. As a result, the standard national language is no longer master in its own home, in its own nation. This affects even the most prominent national languages of the world, such as German. It has become "a disappearing 'small' language (like Breton or Occitan)," writes one of the leading German philosophers of language, Jürgen Trabant. He explicitly calls this sociolinguistic process "revernacularization" and compares its result to medieval Europe, with English instead of Latin in the role of the universal language of the elites and the declining standard national languages as new vernaculars. Even the oldest and the strongest cultural languages and nations of Europe have found themselves in this condition, which Trabant defines as "neomedieval diglossia," at the outset of the 21st century.[5] Anderson, who is fully aware of this new condition, at least in terms of the domination of English as "a kind of global-hegemonic, post-clerical Latin," does not really reflect upon it and its repercussions for his theory of the nation and the international world.

4.2

As mentioned before, Anderson also ignores the process of standardization of national languages, which has additionally made him blind to social and linguistic transformations that give us an essentially different picture of modern history and the role nations and nationalism play in it.

As the title of his book *The End of Standard Language* clearly states, Dutch linguist Joop van der Horst considers the epoch of the standard European languages to have come to an end.[6] By this epoch, he means the Renaissance, whose end we experience today primarily in the form of a deep linguistic crisis. In the last few decades, he claims, our linguistic culture has been transformed more radically than in the previous five centuries. The linguistic-cultural paradigm has changed, one aspect being the disappearance of standard language.[7] The Renaissance understanding of language was based on the idea that our linguistic praxis is genuinely fragmented, divided into many clearly separated linguistic entities, which we perceive as (national) languages and call French, German, Italian, or Slovenian. In the Renaissance, this view, which implies that languages are countable like apples, was almost completely essentialized and naturalized. It became, so to speak, commonsensical, which is why it so easily suppressed the previous, radically different experience of linguistic praxis typical of the Middle Ages, the paradigm of language as a (vernacular) continuum. "[E]verything that was spoken in everyday life formed a vast continuum of variants throughout the entire then-known world."[8] In such a continuum, there was nothing to be counted. One would constantly encounter linguistic differences, sometimes very big ones, but they were never perceived as borders between languages. It was this perception and not the genuine experience of a linguistic continuum that changed with the Renaissance. From then on, the linguistic landscape was seen as composed of different parts, different languages. The standardization of the vernaculars was, of course, constitutive of this. Essentially, it was nothing but the practice of fencing off these new linguistic entities, now imagined as separate languages. This fully applies to national languages as we still see them today: distinct linguistic entities we can count. "They are, and will (for the most part) remain, ideals, fictions. A countable fiction," concludes Van der Horst.[9] He argues, however, that this epoch is over. Today, a reverse process is taking place, albeit one wholly different from Trabant's revernacularization. For Van der Horst, European languages increasingly lose the quality of being countable. The homogeneous, enclosed linguistic unities are falling apart, dissolved in a plethora of new variants. There is no longer one single English; there are many Englishes. The boundary that had maintained the unity of English is crumbling.

There are many reasons for this development: one of them, Van der Horst states, is an overall democratization of modern industrial societies. In the Netherlands, for instance, some 60 percent of those who used to be silent in public space are now talking. The standard language has become everybody's business. If we add to this that instruction in the so-called mother tongue is increasingly losing the social prestige and student interest it enjoyed before and think of mass immigration and the growing number of citizens who are not native speakers of the language-of-state, we are obviously witnessing a new historical trend, quite different from Anderson's projection of a still-developing world of nations. It seems Van der Horst is right. The old vernacular continuum is being slowly but steadily restored. Yet, the question of what this social and linguistic transformation means politically remains.

4.3

Before we try to draft a possible answer, let us devote our attention to one more, no less dramatic linguistic transformation generated by current technological developments. Although it offers yet more proof of the decline of standard national languages, or even of the unavoidable death of many of them, it is still perceived and presented in the fiction of their countability. I'm talking of the so-called digital extinction of languages.

A recently published study by META-NET, titled "Europe's Languages in the Digital Age," reports on the state of thirty—including twenty-three "official"—European languages regarding language technology.[10] As we know, such systems primarily rely on statistical methods that require huge amounts of written or spoken data to feed machine translation services, spell and grammar checkers, et cetera. The problem is, however, that languages with relatively few speakers cannot acquire the mass of data needed. They are, therefore, considered "data-poor" or "low-resource" languages. To put the study's results in a nutshell, a total of twenty-one of the thirty languages analyzed were placed in the lowest category— "support is weak or non-existent"—in at least one area by the experts. While no language was considered to have "excellent support," only English was assessed as having "good support," followed by languages such as Dutch, French, German, Italian, and Spanish with "moderate support." Languages such as Basque, Bulgarian, Catalan, Greek, Hungarian, and Polish exhibit "fragmentary support," placing them in the set of high-risk languages, too. When it comes to the future, the study's verdict couldn't be clearer: most European languages are unlikely to survive in the digital age. How then shall we speak of an alleged equality of national languages, national cultures, and, finally, of nations and believe, as Anderson does, in a still-developing international world?

5

Let us try to sum up the significance of these examples, including the most sinister one: the perspective of a very likely digital death of most European national languages. While Trabant and Van der Horst understand the process of revernacularization in a diametrically opposed way—the former as a historical regression, the latter as a progressive move forward—they agree that standard national languages are increasingly losing their very content. They become "dead, thing-like shells," to use Mikhail Bakhtin's phrase for words or discourses that fall victim to standardization, that is, get caught and reified in grammatical structures.[11] No wonder, then, that Van der Horst also quotes Bakhtin in his diagnosis of the end of standard language:

> The new cultural and creative consciousness lives in an actively polyglot world. The world becomes polyglot, once and for all and irreversibly. The period of national languages, coexisting but closed and deaf to each other, comes to an end. Languages throw light on

> each other: one language can, after all, see itself only in the light of another language. The naïve and stubborn coexistence of "languages" within a given national language also comes to an end—that is, there is no more peaceful co-existence between territorial dialects, social and professional dialects and jargons, literary language, generic languages within literary language, epochs in language and so forth.[12]

It looks like nations are dying, or, more precisely, they are becoming, like their standard languages, dead, thing-like shells, emptied of the imagined content once stored and reproduced in their allegedly unique languages. But does this mean that the force of imagination that had put them on the map is also fading? Are we witnessing today the final moments of imagined communities?

The global rise of nationalism, especially of its increasingly violent, xenophobic, ultraconservative, and even fascist forms, seems to disprove this claim. Yet, what distinguishes today's mobilization of nationalist ideologies and political forces is their radically different global context, the role they play, and the site they occupy. Simply put, the new nationalisms no longer act on the stage of an international world. Rather, they have become instrumental in the reproduction of global neoliberal capitalism as a major ideological and political means for creating and maintaining class structures and power relations—that is, mechanisms of exploitation and domination. To perform this role, such a new nationalism must abandon the task of nation formation, evacuate the fictional center of the national community—where the old one had imagined its cultural substance—and move to its borders. Not to demarcate and guard an exclusive national sovereignty against others, but to keep global capitalism going and its beneficiaries, its ruling classes, in power. This is what the borders in today's global world are for. Far from being obstacles to free movement, as liberal minds want us to believe, promising to (democratically) bridge them in the interest of all, they are tools of differentiation and weapons of extermination in the hands and interest of the elites ruling the global world. What once was a sovereign nation in its own state, claiming equality with other sovereign nations and their states within an international world order, has long since died out. Nevertheless, it has found an afterlife.

A nation of today is a zombie-nation, essentially a border creature, a role in which its imagination is turning our reality into horror. Its nationalism does not seem to have lost any strength, either. On the contrary, it has been resurrected as the crucial actor in the violent processes of bordering the world, in cutting continuities of solidarity and emancipation, in nipping in the bud any claim to a common cause beyond identitarian divisions, and in securing the free passage of capital and its global agents, while at the same time fencing off, taming, and distributing its slaves. This leads us back to the crucial metaphorical link between nationalism and language Anderson repeatedly insists on in his book (*IC*, 196).

6

The fact that, so many years after *Imagined Communities*'s first publication, Anderson devotes his afterword to translation—of all the book's topics—indicates much more than a report of his book's translational journey of the world. The afterword is, in fact, a self-critique of the book and, at the same time, the preface to its imagined sequel. In both cases, the focus is on translation.

What Anderson calls vernacularization, praising its emancipatory agency while ignoring its oppressive mechanism, is closely related to the question of property. He explicitly holds the lexicographic revolution—his euphemism for standardization—in Europe responsible for creating and spreading the conviction that languages were the personal property of specific groups—concretely, of nations (*IC*, 84). This is true, but how did grammars and dictionaries actually do this? By cutting the vernacular linguistic continuity into pieces, that is, by fencing off one language from another. There is only one proper name for this: the enclosure of the linguistic commons. Translation, or, more precisely, a particular understanding of translation, played a crucial role in this process. By allegedly situating itself somewhere in between two separate languages, so as to bridge linguistic differences and restore broken communication, it creates the effect of bordering, the impression that two separate languages had already existed as such before translation arrived on the scene. In this view, translation is activated only at the outer fringe of language, where it is supposed to build bridges to another, foreign language. This is precisely how Anderson understands it. For him, translation is a vehicle that carries his book across linguistic, cultural, and political borders. The metaphor of travel is especially seducing. It makes his ideas appear as heroes of a road movie that, despite all the obstacles, distances, and differences, happily arrive at their destination anywhere in the international world.

However, what we miss in this picture are even the least traces of the former linguistic continuity, the legacy of the vernacular commons. We also miss another, radically different understanding of translation, one that sees it in the midst of our linguistic praxis, beyond the borders between languages and before the fiction of separate, clearly distinguishable—and countable—linguistic entities has been established. We miss the idea of translation as a generative force of the—linguistic, cultural, social, and political—commons. Such an idea has, of course, consequences for our understanding of "universality."

Imagined Communities knows two notions of universality. The first, already mentioned in the second sentence of the introduction, refers to "the formal universality of nationality as a socio-cultural concept," which Anderson sees in a paradoxical contradiction to "the irremediable particularity" of its concrete manifestations (*IC*, 5). Universality is therefore intrinsic to the concept of nation, but only within the unsolvable paradox of its simultaneous particularity. The second notion of universality is rather historical and refers to "the universality of Latin in medieval Western Europe" (*IC*, 40). Anderson obviously means the universality articulated within the old sacred languages, in contrast and contradiction to the new vernaculars, to which he implicitly ascribes intrinsic particularity. Yet, in both cases, there is no hinting whatsoever toward the possibility that vernacular continuities might also claim some sort of universality. Although fully aware of the radical change in property relations implied in vernacularization—read: standardization—that is, of the fact that it brings about a privatization of linguistic praxis by a particular group, a nation, Anderson never asks whose property the linguistic praxis had been before. He is blind to the vernacular commons, to their linguistic, social, economic, cultural, and historical meaning as well as, not least, to their ability to articulate a universality beyond national and nationalistic particularities.

Talking of the universality of Latin in medieval Europe, Anderson does not fail to mention that it "never corresponded to a universal political system" (*IC*, 40). With that, he implicitly claims that the world of nations, which historically replaced the medieval world, is, in contrast, a universal political system. He imagines the world as a community of nations and tacitly accepts the existing international order as the final form of political universality.

But is it really true that "nation" is the last word of our political imagination? What if the narrative force that had once created the nation as an imagined community has moved forward, abandoning its emptied shell? What if it has found an afterlife in another stage of "particular universality," that of normative identity blocks as a postnational form of imagined communities? What actually is the so-called West beyond the narrative of former nations, the ventriloquist of its afterlife? To which political system does it correspond? If it is neither a nation in its state nor a federation of nations, who then is its sovereign? Who rules "the West" if not a king or an emperor? Is it "the people"? Is "the West" a democracy? Have we ever voted for our representatives in its parliament? Have we ever chosen its prime minister or its president in a democratic election? Why then have we given "the West" our consent to make fateful political decisions and even wage wars in our name? Why have we accepted its borders as a "civilizational difference" that divides us from them—in terms of Carl Schmitt's concept of "the political," that is, in the sense of an existential difference between friend and enemy that drives our imagination of political community?[13] Aren't we afraid of its Nazi legacy and even more of its current translation into the language of a permanent war of our "good" against their "evil"? And, finally, why do we keep imagining "the West" as a community? Is the political afterlife of nation a reality or still a dream? Or has it already become a nightmare?

7

This is no longer a critique of *Imagined Communities* but rather a compliment to its author for making these questions unavoidable today. He was right indeed. We will never cease to imagine our communities. The question is: How to do it in a radically different way?

Such an imagination shall depart opposite of where the imagination of nations and identity blocks has brought us, at the opposite side of the state of war in which we are today. The cause of peace can only be meaningfully addressed by imagining a community rooted in the idea of the commons. Translation, again, is the driving force here—in a sense that goes far beyond its linguistic meaning. In every act of translation, we not only restore a broken communication but, in a deeply historical sense, recover those vernacular continuities destroyed by national languages. Moreover, we revive the legacy of the linguistic, social, and cultural commons that once fell victim to the national enclosures. Translation alone has the potential to rearticulate the suppressed experience of being at once singular and common, an experience that opens a radically new horizon of social and political imagination. It is one that goes beyond the quasi-dialectics of universality versus particularity, in both forms addressed by Anderson: the universality of a master language versus the particularity of the vernaculars, and the "particular universality" of a nation within the international world, the logic intrinsic to the concept of sovereignty regardless of whether it is national or postnational. The latter applies to the normative identity blocks constitutive of the so-called multipolar world that will allegedly emerge out of the ruins of the ongoing wars.

Even without explicitly addressing it, Anderson is aware of the primal trauma around which nations are imagined: the enclosure of the commons. This is precisely why he is disgusted by the violent appropriation—privatization—of the products of his own intellectual labor, or, in his words, by the "the ludicrous American insistence on 'intellectual' (!) property rights." He is no less annoyed by the conviction that one can claim languages as the personal property of specific groups—that is, nations.

This shows that a radically different imagination of our communities cannot but challenge capitalist property relations and, in general, actually existing global capitalism as the world system. More concretely, it must critically address and practically confront the constant reproduction of borders within the global commons, not only the existing political borders of nations and identity blocks, but also those of cultural and racial divisions, gender domination, and, finally, class differences. These borders are sites of struggle along which such an imagination can performatively articulate itself, always acting in the name of the irreducible heterogeneity of the global commons.[14] This is why translation is the only language it can speak and understand—its, as it were, mother tongue.

Benedict Anderson, *Imagined Communities: Reflections on the Origin and Spread of Nationalism*, rev. ed. (London: Verso, 2006), 207 (hereafter cited in the text as *IC*).

Walter Benjamin, "The Task of the Translator," in *Illuminations*, ed. Hannah Arendt, trans. Harry Zohn (New York: Schocken Books, 1969), 69–82, here 71.

Nina Čolović, "Psamtik's Children or Which Language Will the Revolution Speak," *Antipolitika: Anarchist Journal from the Balkans* 3 (2023): 159–85, here 172.

Hugh Seton-Watson, *Nations and States: An Enquiry into the Origins of Nations and the Politics of Nationalism* (Boulder, CO: Westview, 1977).

Jürgen Trabant, *Globalesisch, oder was? Ein Plädoyer für Europas Sprachen* (Munich: C. H. Beck, 2014), 92. Unless otherwise noted, all translations are mine.

There is no English translation of Joop van der Horst's book. The title and quotes in English are mine, translated from the Croatian translation (*Propast standardnog jezika: Mijena u jezičnoj kulturi Zapadne Europe*, trans. Radovan Lučić [Zagreb: Srednja Europa, 2016]) of the Dutch original (*Het einde van de standaardtaal: Een wisseling van Europese taalcultuur* [Amsterdam: J. M. Meulenhoff, 2008]).

Ibid., 8.

Ibid., 94.

Ibid., 102.

10 META-NET, "At Least 21 European Languages in Danger of Digital Extinction," press release, September 26, 2012, http://www.meta-net.eu/whitepapers/press-release. The Multilingual Europe Technology Alliance, a Network of Excellence, consisting of sixty research centers from thirty-four countries, is dedicated to building the technological foundations of a multilingual European information society.

11 Mikhail Bakhtin, *The Dialogic Imagination: Four Essays*, trans. Michael Holquist, ed. Caryl Emerson and Michael Holquist (Austin: University of Texas Press, 1981), 355.

12 Ibid., 12. Van der Horst, *Propast standardnog jezika* (see note 6), 204.

13 Carl Schmitt, *The Concept of the Political*, expanded edition, ed. and trans. George Schwab (Chicago: The University of Chicago Press, 2007).

14 See Sandro Mezzadra and Brett Neilson, *Border as Method, or, The Multiplication of Labor* (Durham, NC: Duke University Press, 2013), especially chapter 9, "Translating the Common," 277–312.

Keti Chukhrov

Itinerant Culture

Deconstructing Stereotypes about Modernity

The critique of modernity in post- and decolonial theory is often based on an epistemic distinction between reason and sense, universality and indigenousness, culture and nature, secularity and sacrality, Enlightenment and mythology. The notions representing rationality and universality are ascribed to Western modernity, whereas those denoting sense and mythology are attributed to the Global South, or the Global East.

While it is true that vestiges of the colonial mentality might be the principal cause for assigning these characteristics to the Western and non-Western geographies respectively, critical thought frequently reproduces them when it views reason, Enlightenment, and modernity as cultural concepts valid predominantly for the West. My essay attempts to deconstruct such dichotomies hinging on location and explore potentialities that could surpass geopolitical and geographic determinations.

Consequently, this text asks whether standpoints that attribute the modern or countermodern view to concrete historical periods or civilizational landscapes might not err, even when they rely on evident cultural tendencies or stereotypes. Such stereotypes are well known: traditional cultures do not fit modernity's understanding of temporality, grounded in history, revolution, and event; modernity is determined by the exchange of the old and the new, whereas traditional non-Western cultures rely on transhistorical stillness and permanence without past and future.

In his seminal work *Exhausting Dance*, André Lepecki equates the temporality of modernity with the colonial mentality. He characterizes the temporal paradigm of Western dance and music as the constant pursuit of the lost present moment. Lepecki's main point is that the choreographed and composed temporality of dance (and consequently of the music of modernity) relies on the "now's" eventality (Badiou) passing away; the choreography of modernity stages the grievance over the eluding moment, over the loss of the present. The spell of the kinetic in the performing arts, their motility and chase of fleeting beauty as modernity's frame, arises precisely from the pursuit of the lost object or moment.[1]

This is why the body in the performing arts—choreography, theater, music—has to be artificial, "architectured," and disciplined. It should attain "impossible" skills in the performing arts paradigms of modernity, since it has to perfectly fit the pursuit of the ideal and irretrievable "now" in each moment that this "now" passes by. In this case, we are dealing with a sequence of utmost moments rather than a becoming of the present. Instead of the colonial model of "classical" modernity, Lepecki advocates for an expanded anti-kinetic *durational present without past and future*, without the fleeting moment of the "now," which presupposes a return to stillness and the natural duration of an organism. In short, body and temporality should not be structured; a body should inhabit space and loosely exist in time rather than aspire to reaching a yet unattained goal.

A similar distinction between the temporality of the event and that of stillness is made by Theodor W. Adorno in his *Philosophy of New Music*—with the only difference that his preferences are the other way around.[2] In Adorno's study of *new* music, one of the types of temporality evolves as a revolutionized articulation of the event and its pursuit, as a resistance against the stillness of ontological duration. Such an approach is embodied by Arnold Schoenberg and the New Viennese School. Another approach is traditionalist counterrevolutionary temporality, as exemplified by Igor Stravinsky and featured in the folk music of all nations, as Adorno assumes. The reason he chooses Schoenberg over Stravinsky is that the latter relies on traditionalist paradigms of composition, evading the developmental approach to time. Because of that, many theorists have concluded that Adorno's stance is elitist and Eurocentric.

Adorno's disregard of folk music does not depend on location. He prefers the revolutionary type of temporality because it is characterized by the choice of an idea and its dialectical development in a composition: the musical material itself (its textural parameters) forms an articulate logic, reflects on its own form and thereby surpasses a mere horizontal passage of time. In this musical paradigm, a piece transcends the chronic pace of time, which is its mere adornment and accompaniment, and its organization becomes a speculation on itself.

Thus, Adorno does not criticize folklore as such, but the inability of music to reflect on itself.[3] However, such a reflection is not necessarily confined to a composing subject, as he erroneously assumes. It can often be ingeniously generated by an ensemble in a performance, as is often the case in the ethnic and folk music of any region, be it in the East, South, or West. What is meant is the speculation on the development of musical form, which is inscribed in the musical material by the composer and becomes immanent to it.

Adorno clearly overlooks (allegedly due to insufficient knowledge of non-Western musical traditions) that forming an idea with musical material is not confined to professionally composed music. Folk music actually contains both paradigms he outlines: the one that presupposes stillness (traditional) as well the one that features resistance, development, and tragic or ecstatic climaxes (revolutionary).

Much in the same way, what Lepecki criticizes as the temporality of modernity—pursuit of the event, of the lost moment, or of the precious object, and the intensification of this pursuit in the excessive forms of performative repetition—already characterized ancient Greek tragedy and the myths it was based on. And it occurred well before European modernity. Indeed, modern European music rests upon the establishment of the harmonic minor scale for the opera, which was chosen for its raised seventh and served to represent grief and mourning.

The structural logic of 16th- and 17th-century music had to express the loss of a beloved person—its paradigmatic plot being the myth of Orpheus. Unlike the monotonous, circular form of medieval music, music since the early Baroque (1600) and up to 1910 took on a developing form, leading to a culmination. The Baroque opera adopted the intensity of ancient Greek tragedy.

Yet, the use of a special scale to express pain or grief can easily be found in Indigenous vocal music, too. Modern music had to invent its own tonality, different from that of ancient Greek tragedy, as the latter's musical components did not survive and could be reconstructed only approximately.

This is to dispute Lepecki's dismissal of the pursuit of the lost moment in dance and music, which he predominantly ascribes to modernity: even when music did not rely on the keys traditionally used for mourning—be it the ancient Locrian scale, employed in tragedy, or the harmonic minor of European modernity—it could still articulate grief with its own tonal means, specifically molded for that purpose, and shift away from chronic, static temporality. The desire to express grief and the search for its musical and tonal articulation is thus not confined to a particular location.

In his study of "the rhythm of cultural dynamics" in Europe, Alexander Dobrokhotov shows that certain cultural qualities of modern time—which we predominantly ascribe to the

19th and 20th centuries—can be traced to other periods and landscapes as well, since they share certain attitudes to sociality, tradition, novelties, beliefs, or habits.[4]

For example, the signs of the Enlightenment usually associated with the 18th century can be discovered at the end of the 5th century BCE in the Middle Eastern or Caucasian literary canons. Likewise, the early 20th-century avant-garde, with its rejection of classical forms as well as its denial of mimesis and figurative realism, has analogies in the 1st to 3rd centuries (early Christianity). We see here that the decision in favor of modernity or countermodernity is determined by a desire to overcome a certain stability of social and cultural forms (in the case of modernizing movements) or, on the contrary, to preserve those stabilizing components.

This is to say that a revolutionary gesture suspending a tradition (or a custom) can be performed anytime and anywhere; such a gesture subsists in the denial of religious idols and habits or in the reluctance to comply with the ruling authorities. Hence, a striving toward a modernization that leaps out of the temporalities of permanence and stability might as well be discovered in Indigenous, non-Western, or ancient cultures.

Conversely, the ritualistic attitude to social life practiced in ancient, theocratic, or Indigenous societies is no less prevalent in contemporary business models or new forms of vectoral capitalism[5] than in clerical and fundamentalist communities. An exchange between the adherence to outdated customs and regulations and the abrupt choice of a novelty can be encountered in various parts of the world as well as various epochs and societies. In any social or cultural experience, there is something that replaces the status quo and something that remains intact.

At times, what supersedes the tradition might be more emancipatory than what stays the same.

To Borrow from Empire

Thus, the concept of modernity acquires historical and geopolitical relativity, whereas the concept of culture, usually associated with a particular identity or period, reveals its nomadism. A good example of cultural nomadism is the so-called Graeco-Arabic translation movement, which emerged in the 8th century in the Islamic Golden Age, during the Abbasid period (750–1258). It initially developed as an echo of Hellenism but later became an autonomous Arabic humanities school. Eventually, it expanded the zone of secular intellectual creativity in the Islamic world and considerably influenced the Christian countries, which had limited opportunities to circulate ancient Greek texts because of clerical regulations.

The center of the movement was the House of Wisdom—a library established in Baghdad at the end of the 8th century, gathering translators of both Muslim and Christian denominations and initiating translations from Greek, Persian, and Sanskrit. Among the conspicuous representatives of the movement were Hunayn, his son Ishaq Ibn Hunayn, his nephew Hubaysh Ibn al-Hasan al-A'sam, and colleague Isa Ibn Uahya.

It should be noted that some texts by Aristotle, Plato, as well as Plotinus and other Neoplatonists only became accessible in the Caucasus—Georgia in particular—because of these Arabic translations. The Byzantine clerical culture of the time was not interested in the proliferation of pre-Christian thought. Moreover, it is through the Arabic and Persian poetry written between the 9th and 12th centuries that Neoplatonism influenced the emergence of the poetry of courtly love in medieval Europe (Languedoc). The same goes for the Georgian poetic tradition, located at the crossroads between West, South, and East. Georgia's main literary monument of the 12th century, Shota Rustaveli's *Knight in the Panther's Skin*, would be unimaginable without that influence.

Even more remarkable is the impact of Arabic-Islamic philosophy and Arabic poetry on the motifs and imagery of late medieval and early Renaissance Italian and French poetry. As Samar Attar emphasizes, Petrarch, Guido Cavalcanti, and even Dante would not have been able to develop the theme of venerating a lady associated with divinity without "borrowing from the Arabic and Islamic sources."[6] Dante and Cavalcanti studied under Brunetto Latini, who was quite familiar with Arabic and Islamic works. The adoration of a woman, which was a blasphemy in medieval Europe, came from Arabic poetry and Sufism (for example, Ibn Arabi). As Attar confirms, "the idea that a beloved woman can be the manifestation of divinity or the emanation of God was acceptable among the Arabs much earlier before the thirteenth century."[7] In the Arabic tradition, there was no conflict between human and divine love. The metaphysical dimension of corporeal love also appeared in this context because of translations of ancient Greek Platonic and Neoplatonic texts.

It is probably impossible to find a region that was able to evade the impact of neighboring societies and cultures in the history of humankind. Such an impact might often have the character of an assault or conquest. There are many cases where a colonial state dominates a foreign culture, erasing local languages and customs. But cultural influence might as well be caused by the voluntary aspiration to exceed one's local limitations and study other modes of production and creativity to learn or even borrow from how others live, produce, and interact.

Both the Byzantine Empire and the Arab Caliphate subjugated Georgia—a small, less influential country—in various ways. From the middle of the 8th century, Georgia was part of the caliphate for almost two centuries (in Georgian history, this period is known as the Araboba). The capital Tbilisi was part of an emirate for even longer, until 1122, after David IV "the Builder" won the Battle of Didgori against the Seljuqs in 1121 and reintegrated the city into Georgia, making it the royal seat.

These examples crystallize two seldom-discussed issues: inevitable cultural nomadism and voluntary borrowing from a colonizing culture. My questions here are: Does the colonial pressure Georgia experienced from the Byzantine Empire and the Arab Caliphate cancel the cultural and humanitarian impact Arabic and Greek philosophy and literature might have had on Georgian poetry and thought? Should we give culture, poetry, and thought a space that preserves their epistemological autonomy and aesthetic achievement without completely identifying them with the colonizing state in which they emerged?

Maybe culture and thought function in a dimension that—following Chantal Mouffe's distinction between the *ontics* of real politics and the *ontology* of the emancipatory political horizon[8]—cannot be completely instrumentalized but maintains their emancipatory potential ontologically, culturally, and epistemologically.

Culture Beyond Territories and Geopolitics

In his *Poetics of Relation*, Martinican anti-colonial thinker and poet Éduard Glissant provides an excellent formula for the cohabitation of cultures: he suggests that the opacity of another culture, or of the *other*, is not an obstacle for creating a relation and common fabric out of the difference between them. Togetherness does not contradict distinction. "To feel in solidarity with this other or to build with him or to like what he does, it is not necessary for me to grasp him . . . nor to 'make' him in my image." At the same time, opacity "is not enclosure within an impenetrable autarchy but subsistence within an irreducible singularity. . . . The right to opacity would not establish autism; it would be the real foundation of Relation, in freedoms," writes Glissant.[9]

If he still preserves the *self* as the unit of the cultural landscape—albeit as an opaque one—Vladimir S. Bibler goes even further and argues that culture in its episteme and inception is a dialogue: it cannot profess any authentic identity by definition.[10] Moreover, the dialogue with the *other* is inevitable, as one has no credible identity even within oneself, and hence even with oneself one enters into a dialogue in the role of the other.

In the associative logic of cultural phenomena, Bibler argues, facts or figures belonging to different periods, regions, or landscapes communicate with each other *simultaneously*. Their connection is dialogical: Georg Wilhelm Friedrich Hegel communicates with Sophocles, Dante with Ibn Arabi, Rustaveli with Ferdowsi, Sergei Parajanov with Mykhailo Kotsiubynsky and Sayat-Nova, Andrei Tarkovsky with Pieter Bruegel and Johann Sebastian Bach, Akira Kurosawa with Fyodor Dostoevsky. Culture exceeds ethnography, geography, and folklore.

This dialogue, however, is not a regular conversation. As Bibler contends, it is held not merely between contemporaries but with a *potential* interlocutor "in such a way that s/he should be able to perceive me—even when I disappear from this potential interlocutor's momentary horizon (leave the room, go to another 'polis,' pass away from life). So that the potential interlocutor would perceive 'me' as if from another, infinitely distant world."[11] This means that, potentially, "I" will be speaking after my death, that is, I might need to speak with others of other times and places—from another time, century, landscape, or language. Every culture, therefore, is a kind of "two-faced Janus." "Its face is as intensely turned toward another culture, toward its existence in other worlds, as it is directed into the depths of itself, in an effort to change and complete its being."[12] In such an interpretation, the destiny of a culture is to exist outside its own territory and address another existence.

In Tarkovsky's *Mirror* (1975), the protagonist remembers standing in a snow-covered landscape as a schoolboy and looking down a hill where other children are skating and tobogganing. The image explicitly refers to Bruegel the Elder's winter landscapes. A viewer who has seen these paintings immediately grasps the cultural and poetic association. However, this oblique quotation is not meant to merely demonstrate the landscape's affinity with famous artworks. It is used because there is something in Bruegel's art that exceeds chronic time and place, so that the quoted paintings serve as an imaginary satellite of anyone's reminiscence about winter or childhood.

This supplementary cultural association allows Tarkovsky to elevate an everyday moment into the realm of the eternal. Moreover, such references emphasize the existential dimension of daily experience, common to many, beyond one's lifespan and geographic location. The example perfectly illustrates Bibler's metaphor of culture as Janus-faced. Bruegel's painting has its own specific origin, its site of belonging and peculiar features, but is at the same time open for an encounter with whoever discovers it as an existential event, quite like discovering a message in a bottle in the middle of the sea.

1 André Lepecki, *Exhausting Dance: Performance and the Politics of Movement* (New York: Routledge, 2006), 123–25.
2 Theodor W. Adorno, *Philosophy of New Music*, trans. Robert Hullot-Kentor (Minneapolis: University of Minnesota Press, 2020).
3 Theodor W. Adorno, *Introduction to the Sociology of Music*, trans. E. B. Ashton (New York: Continuum, 1988).
4 Alexander Dobrokhotov, *Filosofiya kultury: uchebnik dlya vuzov* (Moscow: Higher School of Economics, 2016), 363–85.
5 McKenzie Wark, "The Vectoralist Class," *e-flux Journal*, May 2015, https://www.e-flux.com/journal/65/336347/the-vectoralist-class/.
6 Samar Attar, "Divided Mediterranean, Divided World: The Influence of Arabic on Medieval Italian Poetry," *Arab Studies Quarterly* 40, no. 3 (2018): 197–212, here 203.
7 Ibid.
8 Chantal Mouffe, *On the Political* (Abingdon: Routledge, 2005).
9 Édouard Glissant, *Poetics of Relation*, trans. Betsy Wing (Ann Arbor: University of Michigan Press, 2010), 193, 190.
10 Vladimir S. Bibler, *Ot naukoucheniya—k logike kul'tury: Dva filosofskikh vvedeniya v dvadtsat' pervyy vek* (Moscow: Politizdat, 1991), 288. Unless otherwise noted, all translations are my own.
11 Ibid.
12 Ibid.

Milo Rau
in Conversation with
Ekaterina Degot

"What will we say in ten years?"

124

Ekaterina Degot (ED): Presently, the Right is coming to power everywhere. You just announced your next festival, *Republik der Liebe* (Republic of Love), I just finished mine, *Horror Patriae*. Our situations differ somewhat. The Right has not yet been able to form a federal government. Meanwhile, the state elections in Styria promise a landslide for the ultraright Freedom Party (FPÖ).[I]

Our festival this year was pretty combative. On the one hand, the response from local audiences and the press was great, but on the other hand, I received many direct and indirect criticisms or complaints that we are parasites, that we are not loyal, that we are criticizing local patriotism. At some point, the extent to which criticism was prohibited and loyalty expected reminded me of Soviet times. Graz is known in Austria for strategic voting, and the same strategizing is expected in the public sphere: better not to touch upon this or that theme as it will only make things worse, bad people will use it against everybody, et cetera. Therefore, my first question is: In your work at the Vienna Festival, were you asked to self-censor? As in: better not poke the bear, let's do it more mildly—did you ever hear anything like that?

Milo Rau (MR): Yes, I would say all the time, and I'm not talking about social media, but more about, for example, the city parliament. The FPÖ and the Austrian People's Party (ÖVP) are not yet in a coalition, and this might not happen. But just yesterday, the FPÖ candidate for the chancellorship, Herbert Kickl, met with Viktor Orbán and signed the so-called Vienna Declaration, a very different document from the one the Vienna Festival published some months ago. They proclaim an axis—a poignant term in the German-speaking context—along which to deconstruct Europe. This foremost means peace with Russia.

I was attacked almost immediately upon arriving in Vienna, mostly by the national organization of the FPÖ and not so much by the municipal government. The Vienna Festival doesn't depend on the federal government so much, as Vienna is a "red island." Neither FPÖ nor ÖVP have a majority; the city is still ruled by the Social Democrats and the liberal NEOS. In their attacks, the FPÖ especially loves the term "antisemitism," which they've used against writer Annie Ernaux, former Greek Minister of Finance Yanis Varoufakis, and, in the end, even against Israeli-German philosopher Omri Boehm, who is actually an intelligent Zionist of sorts. Perhaps that's very Soviet, that you can use openly fascist terminology and declare others to be fascists.

One of the FPÖ's election promises was to cut subsidies for the Eurovision Song Contest and for the Vienna Festival. So, the battle is still ongoing. I was rereading Václav Havel's writings from the socialist period and discovered that we haven't reached the state he described yet. Perhaps in five years, or perhaps in ten, we will be there.

ED: I came to Graz to run steirischer herbst in 2018; at that time, the FPÖ was already in a coalition with the conservative centrist party—and very present. Despite all its rhetoric, it did not affect the festival in any drastic way back then. Today, many people in Graz think nothing will happen this time either. But I remember how, when Jörg Haider's FPÖ came in second in the 1999 parliamentary elections, the magazine *Camera Austria* appeared with only black pages. This would be a very extravagant and lonely gesture today, which means that the Right has already won—by being normalized. I cannot even say, as Germans do, that it "entered the salons" (*ist salonfähig geworden*), because it never left them. It pulled the center strongly to its side; the conservatives' rhetorical apparatus is sometimes not that different from the right-wingers'. But the Right has won over the Left, too, and reduced its ambitions. Where they agree, interestingly, is in their mistrust of an international festival like ours. Culture should be local: national and traditionalist for the Right, defined by the *freie Szene* (artist-run spaces and initiatives) for the Left. In other words, we are targeted because we are international, and pandering to either side will be of no use, I am afraid.

MR: When I published an open letter with Elfriede Jelinek and others against voting for the FPÖ, most comments were of the sort: "You are an idiot. Why put yourself on the list of signatories? Everybody knows that there are lists of people who will be dismissed when the new government comes to power." At the end of the day, I just don't care. This is a historic moment. What will we say in ten years? What did we do ten years ago? They will not spare us because we are nice; they know who we are, we don't have anything to win. The confusing thing about Austria—and that's still different in Germany, France, and Belgium, where I normally work—is that you can have a fascist president of the National Council. He can declare his appreciation for a Nazi prosecutor general who had dozens of political prisoners killed, but nobody cares. Why do we think democracy is invincible when it has always already been destroyed?

ED: I don't think democracy is invincible. I saw how even the weakest democracy died in Russia. I even witnessed some elements of democracy in the late Soviet Union, in its civil society—limited in agency but strong in principles—and they died rapidly with the advent of the free market and its "invisible hand," which was supposed to arrange everything. So I'm rather used to that dynamic. Democracy is hard work and requires personal involvement; many people all over the world do not have this resource anymore. Partly because, especially in rich countries, they are constantly told the world is doomed and humanity is dying. That brings more of the "Why should I care about anything?" attitude.

Everybody's talking about resisting as a way of changing things, but I do not really like this word. Resisting means not giving in to pressure, spending all available energy on not doing what is expected or asked of you. It means staying put, toiling against a strong wind. Sometimes that is, indeed, the only thing left to do: locking yourself in your toilet. In a strong dictatorship, nonparticipation saves history. But we are not yet in this situation in the West, and "resisting" is too often translated into just repeatedly saying you resist. "Resistance" was not the term the Maquis used for themselves. If one has to do something, then it is fighting, not resisting. And that shifts the focus from "what we are resisting" to "what we are fighting for"; it's not a bad idea to think about that. At the same time, I don't think alarmism is an option. I was an alarmist journalist throughout the 1990s and 2000s in Russia, and, sadly, it brought nothing. What can festivals do to change the situation?

MR: Perhaps I have to describe it in terms of my own trajectory, coming from the Atlantic states to Central Europe in the past year. There is something I call the Atlantic delay. In Western Europe, people really think that democracy is invincible, like in Francis Fukuyama's dream. We have democracy, we have deals, we work together, we share an economy. That's why neither the nation-state nor fascism will come back. Liberalism and the welfare state are strong enough.

Our historical problem is that this is all based on the exploitation of raw materials, as we now discover. These resources are coming to an end—and with them, democracy, the liberal state, the whole idea of progress, an entire civilizational model. This is one huge problem. Western civilization is confronted with the question of its own death and how to deal with it. There is paranoia, there is denial, but there is also the idea that dying could be done nicely; when we are smaller, we can somehow survive as a little island of Slovakia or of whatever. In Central Europe, people are already familiar with nationalism and fascism as a negative response. In Western Europe, people still think that democracy will survive because it's linked to the economy. The European project will die together with Volkswagen, which is why the German state unsuccessfully tries to save it.

Another interesting aspect is the persistence of a new intellectual cordon sanitaire between the two halves of Europe. When Matej Drlička, the director of the Slovak National Theatre, was dismissed, nobody in Vienna talked about it, even though Bratislava is only one hour away. But that is Eastern Europe; they are crazy, they love dictators. The Soviet times are coming back, but that's their story, and we will not be affected by it because an invisible line still exists between us thirty-five years after the end of state socialism. At the Vienna Festival, we collaborate with the Venice Biennale Teatro; they have fascists, too, in Italy, but Italian fascism is, of course, different and somehow funny. Willem Dafoe is still the president of the festival; nobody believes that he will be dismissed in the next five years. You always think: this is the story of Russia, this is the story of Slovakia, this is the story of the Austrians, this is the story of whomever, and, in the end, the Wehrmacht invades ... The invisible Berlin Wall no longer exists to protect anyone.

ED: Yes, the recent election victories of Donald Trump in the US, of the AfD in Germany, and the FPÖ in Austria prove that there is no firewall. The best way to come to power is to be like Vladimir Putin: to allow the rich to get richer and deny the disappearance of raw materials and the harm of resource capitalism. And, by the way, the "extreme center" were Putin's enablers to begin with. We should remember they largely agreed with his earlier version of pseudo-liberal authoritarianism.

MR: In that sense, a certain kind of resistance has already failed. We have already lost the fight against fascism, which has now irreversibly returned to Europe, confirming Marxist laws of history about the economy. To resist its return means denying these laws. There is, however, another kind of resistance one can learn from: resistance within a system you completely deny, as practiced by the Landless Workers' Movement. You occupy a space (even if it is just your toilet) where there is a basic and radical no to fascist capitalism. In Brazil, this involves reclaiming a space from agribusinesses that is the size of a whole country, creating a nation within the nation. It has its own church, its own educational system.

As the whole planet shifts to radical ethnic fascism, what should we do? We could start to create models of the Paris Commune inside of it, rather than taking back power in civil society. If parliament is presided over by a fascist, how can I defend parliamentary democracy? What do we create then? It's a question of what will arise inside the destroyed European empire. What will we construct there? I don't have an answer now, but I look to Brazil or Southern Italy, to spaces where a civilization has already lain in ruins, in the case of Brazil for 500 years. There is one sentence I liked a lot in *Antigone in the Amazon*: Kay Sara, the Indigenous philosopher, saying you have no experience with the end of the world, and we've been experiencing it for 500 years. In Europe, the world is ending now, but in Brazil, they have strategies. The important thing is to make the connection between what is happening now in Austria, or, let's say, Central Europe or Europe in general, and what happened in Russia nearly thirty years ago.

ED: Let's think about it in concrete terms. So, the far right cuts funding, which is a real possibility, even if they don't fire you and me. What can we do? Do you think that some old forms can be revived? I had a journalist friend in Russia who, still in the 1990s, said that if they closed his radio station, he would deliver the news by megaphone to every house. That, unfortunately, did not happen, even if the radio station no longer exists. So, can we return to that? Is some kind of crowdfunding possible? Can we return to apartment exhibitions and illegal performances? Should we think in those directions already?

Or maybe it's important to hang on to these institutions we have? steirischer herbst, for example, was founded in 1968 and has anti-fascism in its DNA, even if some people associate its early years with formalist art. It always represented an attempt to break with the cultural hegemony of ex-Nazis and create something new on a big scale. Shouldn't we hang onto that?

MR: In my inner self, I would be very happy to be marginalized soon. While I enjoy playing with these big institutions (as do you, I guess), I like being on the periphery, doing my stuff in strange surroundings, and creating the kinds of spaces that no longer exist. Because now, I'm experiencing the uncool moment of resistance. I'm saying no, no, no, pushing people back, and reminding them of what we learned in school: we shouldn't use these words, we shouldn't behave like this. This puts me in the uncool position of a teacher. I also have many administrative and representative duties, and that is not really my world. So, it's very beautiful to imagine going this pirate radio way of influencing and making guerilla propaganda from an invisible space.

On the other hand, I am trying to reappropriate this big institution, which, like your festival, also has an anti-fascist past. The problem is more that we, as a cultural elite, have created a distance between civil society and our festival space. This is just how institutions work. It's not that we decided to close the doors or exclude the public.

But we've raised ticket prices, and we have titles so complex that nobody bothers with them. That is just how this milieu developed in the last thirty, forty years, in a civilization like ours. What I am trying to do now (and I guess you are, too) is to allow the media and the public to reclaim the festival, to become popular again.

ED: We are also working in this direction. Thirty or forty years ago, it might have made sense to abandon popular culture, or at least to take a break from it, and to establish a specific space for specific practices. Centrist politicians are happy when you recognizably stick to this. The problems start when you move into their terrain.

In the current festival, we experienced a funny story with a work in public space by Yoshinori Niwa. With the massive help of AI, he created a satirical poster of an archetypal right-wing politician brandishing a sausage, with the slogan *Jedem das Unsere!* ("To each ours!") next to him. He washed this poster day by day, making it disappear on election day. When it was installed, it was immediately covered by the police, who were called, allegedly, by some "concerned" passersby. What they were probably concerned about was a mockery of the Right, but what they could legitimately complain about was, of course, fascism: the words *Jedem das Seine* ("To each his own") were written on the gates of Buchenwald. The poster was later uncovered but also criticized for not being artsy enough, entirely missing the point that the artist was washing it off and making it disappear. What's interesting is how assertive politicians became once we entered public space and used popular language.

MR: That's the only way we can save these institutions. Not that this is such a new idea; it's been clear for fifteen or twenty years that we need to become more popular. There are still people who are trying to cancel everything that is not completely in-line. What I try to do—and this is, of course, also a strategy—is invite everybody to the festival who does not openly call themselves a fascist. Whoever doesn't want to kill me can come, more or less. I invited everybody from the FPÖ. I really tried to be inclusive. And I defend this against my leftist friends who call everybody a racist who does not use exactly the language they would love everybody to use. You have to defend the inclusiveness of this space in all directions. You have to invite right-wing and left-wing people. You have to be popular. If we have one more generation that is bent on canceling, shaming, and excluding people from the leftist scene, then we are really lost. Maybe we are lost anyway, and they will shut down the Internet in five years.

ED: You and I might not be as lost as all that, but the Left certainly is. I experience a complete cognitive dissonance with my left-wing friends who are talking about inclusivity in a language even I do not understand. When I try to change it for publication, they very much resist sinking to that level. With whom are they talking then? At the same time, we have to be against brainless populism.

MR: We are being attacked from that side as well. We, too, are trying to involve people with different positions, such as traditional Austrian marching bands, to create a dialectical contradiction, not just to celebrate marching band music or right-wing positions.

ED: I wanted to ask something else. Recently, you've been making a strong case for placing the emphasis of resistance on our global alliances. I fully agree, but global alliances are endangered now as well. Not only is a new Iron Curtain being raised, which we just spoke about, but there are also new schisms, brought about by competitive traumas, between the historical trauma of the Holocaust, on the one hand, and, on the other, that of colonization and its present form in Gaza and the West Bank. This schism is already making many discussions impossible, while there is still a huge blind spot where the Holocaust and intra-European colonization meet, as the attempt to erase European Jewry went hand in hand with the colonization of lebensraum in Eastern Europe.

In Europe, doing something postcolonial usually translates to doing something fashionably American, where racism is much more about skin color. Locals in Graz might say: "Oh, this is great, it's about slavery, it's very far away." But there is a colonization issue right here vis-à-vis Southern and Eastern Europe, where people have the same skin color. So it's time to talk about intra-European colonization and racism.

MR: When I was in the Austrian Museum of Folk Life and Folk Art in Vienna, where we set up the festival center for the past edition, I went to the basement, and there were a lot of ritual sticks and stuff. I said: "Oh, wow, this is interesting, I guess it's from Mongolia or the Amazon." And they said: "No, it's from here, but it has been erased in the past hundred years." This was Europe before we colonized the rest of the world. And we are still colonizing Europe. Everybody knows what happened during the French Revolution. It was the beginning of democracy, but it also spelled the destruction of Lyon and the North and the South as well. The French Revolution had its own inner genocides. We had to colonize ourselves before we colonized the others.

ED: I must say this argumentation brings a sinister déjà vu to me. If we colonized ourselves, it is time to decolonize, according to current views. "Decolonizing" the "authentic" ritualistic culture—normally, that would be folk culture—means liberating it from modernity, industrialization, cosmopolitanism, internationalism, and all other inauthentic things, including all the mixing of identities. The desire to protect this purity is precisely what brought the *Heimatschutz* movement to life in the late 19th century, a conservative ideological front protective of the "autochthonous" rural way of life that went far beyond culture and left a strong imprint in German and Austrian politics and society. One can even say that, in Austria, it was not discredited by the catastrophe of Nazism but survived and constantly returns with a vengeance. The protectionism that defines the current cultural politics of one part of the Left often resembles this *Heimatschutz*.

MR: Meanwhile, for 18th- and 19th-century Europeans, it was much easier to be enslaved than to enslave somebody else. You just had to choose the wrong route through Turkey and you could be enslaved. Academic discussions in the US are all about the transatlantic slave trade, so it seems absurd to apply them to Central Europe. The story of Black slavery is very relevant to Belgium, France, and England, but the Central European states have a very different history of slavery and bondage.

In France and Belgium, the conflict in the Middle East is interpreted as a colonial war and one of taking land, legitimated by the Zionist complex. In Central Europe, people see it as a conflict of being surrounded by people who hate you and want to erase you. Here, they read it against the backdrop of Holocaust history, while in Western Europe, they read it through the prism of colonization, which is very visible in every family history.

ED: I think we are so in love with the postcolonial stories of the Atlantic and the US because we want to be part of them. It's prestigious: white people have problems with slavery. Central Europeans have Nazis and Communists in every family, victims and perpetrators, or supposedly apolitical bystanders implicated in the horrific events that took place here. It seems safer to talk about the more abstract and distant atrocity of transatlantic slavery and colonialism, and even claim a part of it, than to address the painful and actual history of the region directly, especially if it concerns your grandparents or great-grandparents. It's even easier to forget it all once the relatives who remember it are dead.

MR: Twenty years ago, as leftists and intellectuals, we still had the guilt of the Holocaust. Meanwhile, right-wing parties have appropriated it. The children of the killers are capitalizing the guilt of their grandparents' deeds. The liberal tradition of guilt is going through a strange endgame, in which these different traumas are little more than chips. In Vienna, the FPÖ supports the Jewish community. When I was preparing a staged trial with or around the FPÖ, they were laughing at me and saying: "Milo, we fascists, we understood you should not criticize Israel, and you leftists should also understand it because nobody cares what you really think." I was still raised in a political tradition where what you say and what you think and what is right on a theoretical level should be the same. Yet, we are surrounded by neoliberal Machiavellians who just use whatever wins next week's fight.

Now we come perhaps to the most central question of this whole discussion: What is to be done? When Vladimir Lenin asked this question 120 years ago, his answer was: "I don't believe in the motions of history anymore, everything is chaotic; we just need a small group of people who will seize power, and then we will change society." This was, as we know, the downfall of the 20th century.

ED: I guess you are referring to Lenin's distrust of trade unionism and working-class spontaneity. In the late 19th century, when Friedrich Engels was still alive, it seemed like these would inevitably triumph, but by the time World War I broke out, the Second International fell apart. Lenin said there needed to be a cadre of professional revolutionaries, and he was right: the relatively small but disciplined Bolsheviks achieved a revolution in the huge Russian Empire. Steve Bannon admires that. But unlike Bannon, Lenin was no cynic; he believed in the great movement of history, just as he believed that the political mass movements of his time in politics had lost touch with it. One might say something similar of center-left liberalism today. Victory seemed inevitable, yet now we have Trump in the White House, who appears to have told the American people what they want to hear.

MR: This is exactly the strategy of the Right. They say: "We don't believe in anything anymore. We take this, we take that. But what we want is to take power—and then change the system in such a way that nobody else can come into this position anymore." That's all they are interested in. And I only started to understand this in Vienna. Because, with the Atlantic delay, in Belgium and France, you still think you are defending culture and society at large, the history of humanity. In Austria, the Right will say whatever it takes to stay in power forever. There is no truth anywhere. There is a beautiful saying about the

Austrians: they are the only people who get more stupid with experience. It is usually attributed to Karl Kraus, a genius in a country of so many genius writers. The multiethnic, polyglot country in which this saying emerged is gone, unfortunately.

1 The conversation took place on October 30, 2024.

Ranjit Hoskote in Conversation with David Riff

The Reinvention of Cosmopolitics

David Riff (DR): To start, we might compare notes on our respective situations. In Europe, we can see the broad resurgence of the ultraright today, which is poised to enter coalitions in Germany and just celebrated a resounding election victory in Austria.[1] All of this has a huge impact on the cultural world, where funding becomes a political issue and a way of reining people in, cutting them down. We know that museums, funding bodies, and festivals are all under attack, with the ultraright demanding their "repositioning." How is the situation in India? I've read that Narendra Modi, although still in power, now faces growing resistance.

Ranjit Hoskote (RH): There are many points of similarity between the European situation and the Indian one—as well as situations elsewhere in the world. Take this week's fiasco in Seoul, for instance, where a wannabe dictator and his *milites gloriosi* thought they could join the global mainstream of tyranny with impunity. Fortunately, they were pushed back hard by an angry and determined coalition of legislators and the people at large. For me, all these situations revolve around the collapse of what we used to imagine being the centrist ground of reason and its potential to shape and support some form of commonality. That was probably an illusion altogether. We should have known this in India, because we saw it happening as early as 1977, toward the end of the Emergency, when Gandhian centrists and socialists made common cause with right-wing parties, who weren't yet over-ground. There was a long proscription on them during the Nehru period and much odium attached to them after. It was the Gandhian centrists and the socialists who returned them to respectability. We have seen how those in power were willing to make compromises with the Right, and that's a long history that's come back to bite our bum now. Because in several crucial states such as Bihar, you have the same kind of coalition: old Lohiaite socialists making common cause with the Rashtriya Swayamsevak Sangh (RSS), the ultraright party. In the Gangetic belt, it has been easy to slip from a linguistic Hindi nationalism to a religious Hindu nationalism over a century.

Another superset of problems within which to see this is that I don't know who "the people" are anymore. There was a time when we spoke fairly confidently in the name of the people: the people will know what's best; the people will see through this crisis. We invested our emotional and intellectual energies in the working class or some other social bastion of resistance. The tragedy of the last ten years in India is that we've seen how very brittle and fragile all these constructions are. We've realized there were many people whose social and economic problems should have appealed to the Left, but who were disenfranchised, who felt left out. In India, this is happening with traditionally disenfranchised communities such as the Dalits, for instance, or the so-called Adivasi—a relatively recent term for the marginalized and often historically persecuted aboriginal communities, the so-called Scheduled Tribes. These vulnerable and marginal groups are also moving rightward, not only on their own, but as a result of a long-term agenda of engagement from the Right. From the right-wing standpoint, they're being "brought home" to the Hindu fold—although Hinduism was never quite their home, or, at best, it was a home in which they had to "know their place," a very subservient place. A number of these communities are now going along with the ascendant Right because they don't see any viable opposition.

That brings us to the third motif here: we've not really been able to create a language of inclusiveness from a leftist perspective. Particularly in India, you begin to see that the left leadership has been largely confined to either the Anglophone classes or the people who belong to the intellectual, cultural, social elite, who've extended themselves in a certain way but clearly have not managed to effect major change or create this inclusive language.

DR: What role do cultural institutions play in all of this? When you say you don't know who the people are anymore, did cultural institutions have any sort of broader, popular, democratic, nonelite role? At the moment, we hear all over the world that culture is purely the domain of the elites and a kind of hobby of "woke" academics creating their alternate reality. But surely, it was quite different at some point. In postwar Europe, for example, there was this incredible attachment to cultural institutions as the site of the emergence of bourgeois politics, which now turns out to be increasingly empty.

RH: Right from the 1930s through to the 1980s, we had an amazingly vibrant print media scene, despite colonial-era and then colonial-style legislation that tended to curtail it. There was an extraordinarily large number of journals, little magazines, pamphlets, broadsides, a whole range of publications that kept voices of dissent not only alive but also in the mainstream. This is something I miss today, even though we now have the net, where all of these things could have assumed different avatars.

The other important point is that this vast spectrum of offerings in the print media spanned across languages. Far more people then were at least bi-, if not multilingual. As intellectuals, they participated in different linguistic and literary scenes. For instance, there would be intellectuals who could write in English and Marathi, or English and Hindi, or English and Bangla, and so on. We have been divided into islands and rendered far weaker by the peculiar monolingualism that's come to be more and more a feature of our linguistic and cultural scene.

DR: I guess the cookie-cutter modernity of neoliberal globalization created a kind of spatial cosmopolitanism. But this mode is mute and pretty much illiterate. Elevator music and soothing mantras will do. There is no space for print media. They are hard to maintain online, where spewing hate is much easier. I wonder where, then, the space for an alternative can be staked. You've talked in the past about a possible non-neoliberal cosmopolitics. Where do you see the space or place for that, outside the vanished print media?

RH: It's the main question today: Where do we form institutions that can operate across languages and keep alive this notion of cosmopolitics? How are we going to fight our regional struggles here? How do we retrieve the solidarities that we had? We felt for a long time that we had close affinities with colleagues elsewhere. To me personally, that's a significant theme. It's not about taking pride in a supposedly cosmopolitan ability to be at home everywhere. Rather, it's the possibility for us to reach out to other predicaments in a very definite way and release ourselves to them, in a generative spirit of solidarity. To me, this is the basis of a robust and lively cosmopolitanism. It is not a universally executable program that unfolds in various locales, but something that we form between locales.

DR: Precisely that seems more and more challenging. Ideologically, a new autarchy is not only defining the Right, but also strongly present on the left, where the talk of the intersectionality of struggles and solidarity between them has faded into the background, where it's all about sticking to one's own lane and talking about one's own experience. In defining what you call cosmopolitics, what points of reference are there?

RH: I am, of course, drawing upon my childhood and adolescent experience of growing up in a nonaligned country. Part of that experience was about connecting and forming a solidarity across national borders, a global constellation of nations and peoples who had the same experiences of anti-colonial struggle, which still continued during my childhood in the 1970s. These were societies that had rejected both great powers of the Cold War, but other than that, there wasn't a program that had already been created and was being played out.

One of the assumptions of the Non-Aligned Movement, even if it wasn't articulated in quite this way, was that you would release yourself to the vulnerability of the other—a very Levinasian idea, in a strange way—and that we would work together to see what, in fact, we had in common and how we could create a new future together. But it was a work in progress, involving the affective and intellectual labor of figuring out how to craft and frame arguments concerning the planetary future from where we were. And it included learning how, despite economic lack and political weakness, we could extend ourselves toward one another through forms of understanding and hospitality.

I think these remain crucial themes for a cosmopolitics we could phrase today. We don't decide in advance what interests we have in common. We recognize affinities of predicaments and struggle through them, framing a language in which to discuss these shared concerns to form a common though not dogmatically immutable front. It seems to me that these affective energies of being invested in vulnerability and seeking forms of hospitality go against the cookie-cutter, ready-made cosmopolitanism one is usually presented with.

The question is: How do you find yourself in the world? How do you make yourself at home in the world? The world is a vexed and turbulent place. The home you're going to make there is not a zone of comfort that remains constant, whether you're in Boston or London or Berlin or Nairobi or Delhi or Jakarta. You will have to craft it afresh. So, this idea of home is necessarily premised on its not already being a comfortable place. It's premised on crafting that condition of home together with others.

DR: I agree, all the more because we see how dangerous this conflation of home with security can be. In the German-speaking context, we know how toxic *Heimat* can be, and how criticizing it or making light of it is perceived as a stab to the heart of national identity. This *Heimat* is always *unheimlich*, "unhomely," uncanny to begin with, so I like that you embrace that. Home does not have to be comfortable in that way.

But getting back to our conversation, where do you see the space for cosmopolitics, also vis-à-vis the semi-abandoned public institutions? What models should we be drawing upon?

RH: There are plenty of cosmopolitical initiatives in discursive contexts and the activities of people like ourselves. But in what way can we connect these to a more material, productive, and active politics? I don't have an answer to that, but there is something forensic to the search for spaces and allies. This is going to become more urgent and more necessary as we go along. The forms in which we convene will always be episodic and fragmentary, but they can leave behind meaningful residues for further thought and action.

In previous times, there were annual events such as the World Social Forum, which came out of the environmental movement and the Latin American struggles against dictatorship. Other such gatherings also came out of the left of the environmentalist movement and drew on the imagery and actuality of what were then called "people's movements." That's an ancestry to call upon, but it still means that we need to develop these alliances, not just as strategic but as empathetic ones, with people who are involved in struggles on the ground for forest or water rights, for instance. The gap between us and them has widened in recent years, a gap exacerbated by the workings of global capital and its extractive networks. Although we all make efforts to bridge it in seminars and conferences, it needs to play out much more on the ground.

When I was a student, we were so caught up with the great agitations of the day. A major commitment, for my generation, was toward the Narmada Bachao Andolan, a huge people's movement to stop a dam that would have destroyed the livelihood and lands of millions of people. I don't see that kind of large-scale theme that can cut across classes and generations in India today. It's not as if such problems don't exist. But somehow the mechanisms we had to bring people together are absent, or they've been weakened. By this, I mean organizations that sought to connect students with activists, journalists, and political scientists in a zigzagging way. Those zigzagging, intergenerational connections are rather weak now. Within these organizations, you could find people belonging to four or five different generations. Today, particularly in the best universities in India, students have no friends much older than themselves, apart from the occasional and almost formally defined "mentor." Their friendships are horizontal. Since they don't really know anyone who's older than them, the histories, narratives, and struggles that preceded them are all either folkloric or very remote. There's been a general muting of dissent, too. Just before the pandemic, there was a huge moment of public unrest in India. I'm amazed at how the chaos of the pandemic years offered those in power a very efficient camouflage, under cover of which to turn a public health crisis into a permanent emergency whose terms allow all dissent to be silenced at executive will.

DR: The pandemic was a rehearsal for securitization in Europe as well. Here, it very much helped to create a ubiquitous bunker mentality. The Left wants safe spaces, the Center believes it has a firewall against the Right, which, in turn, dreams of Day X and the end of the world. What seems to unite all sides of the political spectrum is this prepper mentality, backed by a deeply idealist belief that there is some lost paradise of harmony and equity to which we should all return.

I wonder whether it doesn't also taint the image of cosmopolitics as we've been discussing it so far. To me, the possible space of cosmopolitics is something more uneven and antagonistic. Solidarity can only arise where people are trying to survive together by coming to arrangements, by doing business, by recognizing common concerns but also different agendas. There has to be disagreement. Centrist governments eagerly eliminate precisely such spaces by censoring certain topics altogether, thus canceling the mere possibility of cosmopolitical dialogue.

RH: I know I tend to give cosmopolitics a rather utopian coloring. But cosmopolitics can only truly be itself, for me, if it is fundamentally linked to releasing oneself to the vulnerability of the other, taking on board the anxieties of the other, embracing a difference you would never want to erase or eliminate. Looking back at these historical experiences in South Asia, we discover, implicit in them, the challenge of finding ways of living and working together despite sometimes radical differences.

So how do you form ways of being together, of communion, of a social harmony that unites people while allowing for spaces where they can be apart, even radically so? One way of thinking about it might be a cellularity of experience: it's not that everyone participates in the same wonderfully joyous, common experience; it also means respecting these differences, which sometimes you may not understand, may not sympathize with, but agree to set aside or accept or account for in a certain way. An example would be the texture of South Asia's encounter with what's generically called uppercase "Islam," but which could more productively be seen as an ensemble of lowercase "islams" that came into the country and were often refashioned here. Was there tension during this process, between incoming and preexisting religions? Certainly. Was there conflict? Certainly. But were there also syncretism, dialogue, borrowing, adaptation, shared festivity? Of course, but those are not the aspects that ideologues of the Right currently choose to remember. And they are being erased from public memory. We are being encouraged to forget that, for instance, with the Mughals, there were amazing moments when people translated each other's work across religious and linguistic lines, sometimes reluctantly and sometimes enthusiastically, almost always being richly transformed by this act. Reluctance and discomfort are also aspects of this larger scenario of learning to live together. We can't just toss out all these conviviality models as being utopian. We accept, of course, that there was conflict and violence as well; these wouldn't be human interactions otherwise, and they need to be discussed in their complex, palimpsestic, open-ended largeness.

Let us not forget that, even in the most difficult historical moments, we had serious and productive discussions across religious or sectarian lines. We're somehow forgetting that. Indeed, we are now even beyond polemics and have entered a phase of mutual annihilation. That is why it is all the more crucial to recall the practice of irenics, a form of dialogue based on achieving peace, accomplishing an ecumenical understanding without erasing difference. However optimistic this might sound in these troubled times, we need to create languages of communion.

DR: That might be, but the worst possible thing is when the state intervenes and starts to protect and regulate these discussions. The German parliament just passed a resolution to "protect Jewish life." This, again, is symptomatic of a "safe space"-based politics, in which the public sphere becomes a securitized wasteland. You yourself were targeted in a larger campaign against Documenta, whose finding committee you were on, and accused of antisemitism because you signed a petition against an Israeli-Indian friendship event organized by Hindu nationalists and right-wing Zionists.

RH: Honestly, I couldn't believe it was happening. To be accused of antisemitism is a truly monstrous charge. As I sat down and drafted a response, I began to think of how sad it was that Germany claimed a monopoly on speaking about Jews, for Jews, about Jewishness, about Judaism, the whole of it. I've never felt so oddly singled out in terms of location. This was not even an undertone, but something fairly explicit in the manner in which the German commentariat addressed me: "If you're Indian, you don't understand these questions." To me, this is absurd, not only because we in India have always had a strong link to West Asia and the Levant, but also because of my personal connections with these supposedly purely European histories, for instance, through my Viennese-Jewish great-aunt Kitty Shiva Rao, née Verständig. On all these levels—intimate, familial, public, historical—I have so many connections with this world and this complex history that it felt bizarre to be not only excluded from this discussion, but considered to have somehow ignorantly questioned some great taboo. It threw into high relief the strange inability of Germany's intellectual class to get past the fact that the reason one needs to remember and never forget the Holocaust is not because it was a unique event, but because it is so horribly, horribly repeatable. It has been repeated over and over again against all kinds of people in all kinds of places as a protocol of annihilation.

DR: One scary aspect of the vision behind this is that the public sphere is evacuated in a permanent emergency, as there is no common ground. All life takes place in its own securitized frame of "Jewish life," "German life," "Turkish life," "Gujarati life," "Marathi life." This seems to point toward a future where autonomous communities live according to their laws in some loose confederation. Is the only space for cosmopolitics between them, then? All these problems with culture and its current vulnerabilities are paralleled by the larger crisis of the universalist nation-state. Should we embrace this future of autonomous communities or reject it? It seems to me to dangerously lead toward notions of purity.

RH: In India, postcolonial modernity—as legislated in a mostly top-down and at that point necessary manner by the 1950 Constitution—precisely marked a transition from a scenario where various religions and castes were more or less governed by their own laws to this idea of a universal set of laws and a state that would offer emancipation to those historically marginalized and persecuted. So, it's not really viable, in an Indian context, to think about autonomous communities that could then interact with one another in some way, especially if their forms of interaction were mediated through the mechanisms of caste. We've done that for hundreds of years, and it's not been a notably successful experiment.

The problem is that each of these communities develops its own inner hierarchy and exceptionalism. We've had far too much of that exceptionalism based on caste or religion or ethnicity in India, which is exactly why, in the early 1950s, this notion of a nation-state seemed such a site of hope and liberation. But we have to seek some mesorealm between the two and think about forming communities not based on primordial identity, ethnicity, religious lineage, whatever it might be—about finding ways of navigating between the nation-state and the crucibles of emergent, ideally self-chosen communities.

DR: I guess it's also a practical question. Should we abandon public institutions or hold onto them?

RH: Although it seems so hopeless at this point, we certainly cannot vacate public institutions in India. That'd be a serious mistake. It's through them that we can still hope to reach people who are not yet citizens, before they are turned into unquestioning subjects. If we vacate those spaces, we could just as well go off into some monastery in the mountains. We cannot lose faith in the idea of renovating the public sphere.

DR: How do you see the role of cultural producers in that regard? Do we have to rethink whom we're addressing and how we're addressing them? The accusations of elitism will always remain, but isn't there a need to rethink what we imagine as intellectual culture and to make it—or maybe to return to a broader view to make it—more accessible in the way that Honoré de Balzac is accessible? I guess a lot of the stuff we're producing today rather isn't. How do you see that?

RH: This question has haunted me as well. We tend to be seen as gatekeepers, but how do we keep these gates open? How do we open ourselves to new audiences? My experience as a writer or organizer of festivals, symposia, and exhibitions is that there actually is a far larger audience, especially young people. They do want to participate in bigger questions, and they don't necessarily want things dumbed down. They're willing to engage. So, it's an artisanal, a practical question: How do we create forms of cultural participation? What are they and where are their entry points?

DR: Do you see any historical precedents where such a broadening and opening succeeded, in a particularly cosmopolitical direction?

RH: Earlier, I spoke of the Progressive Writers' Movement, which was very widespread. Its dominant representatives wrote in

Urdu and Hindi, but their influence was also felt in other languages. Many of them came to Bombay to work in the movies, writing scripts, dialogues, lyrics. And they were able to create a cinema that did not compromise on quality. This popular culture played an important role in the evolution of a popular sensibility between the 1940s and the 1970s. There are, for instance, songs that many of us still sing because their lyrics were written by major poets such as Sahir Ludhianvi, Kaifi Azmi, and Gulzar. It's unbelievable: major Urdu writers who also wrote for the movies. I don't know how this is to be reenacted today. Maybe it can't be recreated in a program; it has to emerge organically from within the cultural field. At some point in our conversation, I expressed my doubts about who or what the people are today. Perhaps we never really knew the answer to that question. Perhaps all we ever did was throw out the first line of a song and hope it would be answered in the same key, in the same spirit, and so on, until there was enough of a critical mass for the song to become an anthem.

1 The conversation took place on December 7, 2024.

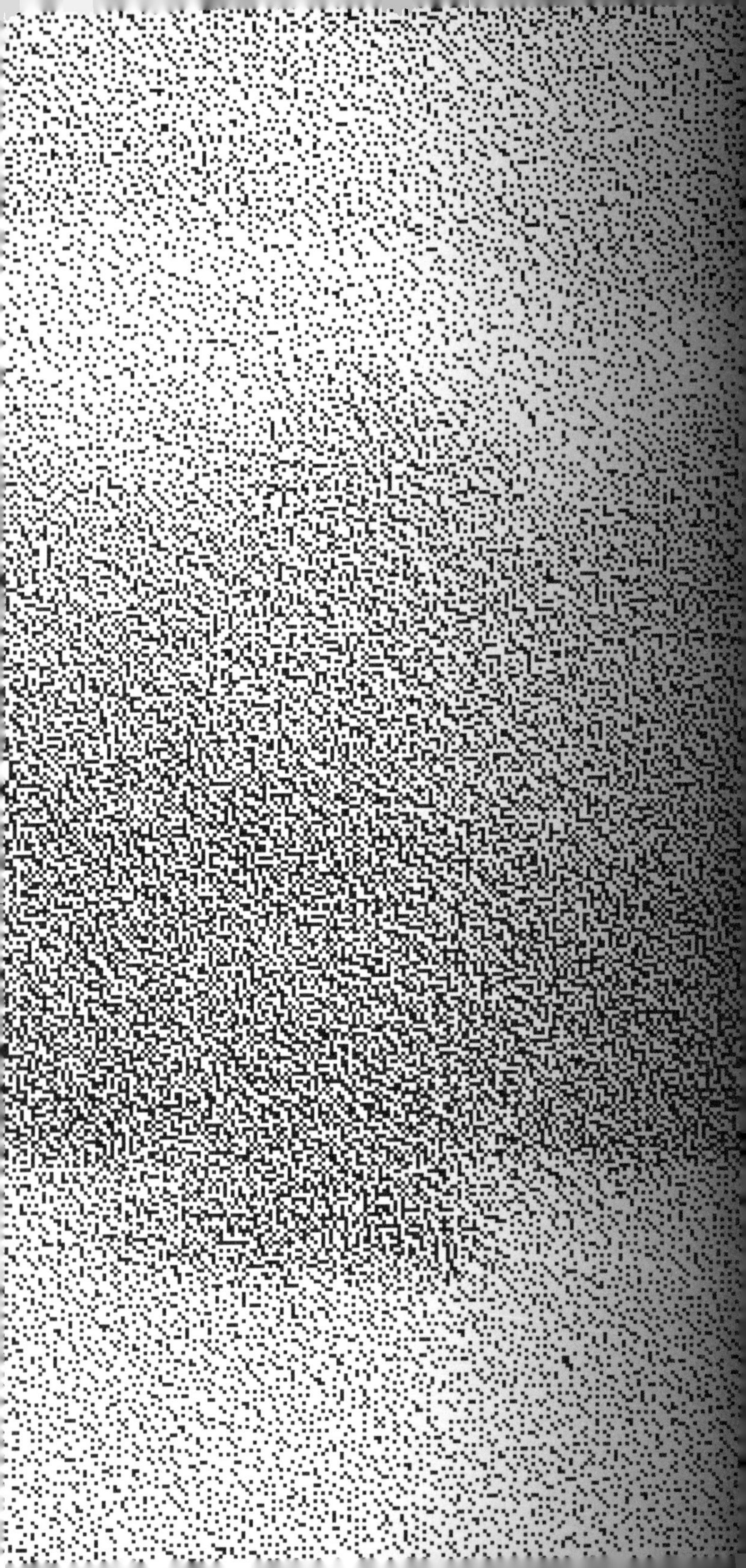

Editors’ Biographies

Ekaterina Degot is an art historian, researcher, and curator focusing on aesthetic and sociopolitical issues in Russia and Eastern Europe from the 19th century to the post-Soviet era. She began her tenure as director and chief curator of steirischer herbst in 2018. From 2014 to 2017, Degot was artistic director of the Academy of the Arts of the World in Cologne. Among other shows, she cocurated the First Ural Industrial Biennial in Yekaterinburg (2010, with Cosmin Costinas and David Riff) and headed the first Bergen Assembly with David Riff (2013).

David Riff is a writer, translator, artist, curator, and former member of the art group Chto Delat. He has been a curator at steirischer herbst since 2018. Among other shows, Riff cocurated the First Ural Industrial Biennial in Yekaterinburg (2010, with Cosmin Costinas and Ekaterina Degot) and headed the first Bergen Assembly with Ekaterina Degot (2013). He continues to translate and artistically address the work of Soviet aesthetic philosopher Mikhail Lifshitz, about whom he curated a large-scale exhibition in Moscow (2018, with Dmitry Gutov).

Contributors' Biographies

Boris Buden is a philosopher and cultural critic. His work focuses on the drastic, often violent historical transitions after the fall of 20th-century socialism and problems of cultural translation. His books include *Der Schacht von Babel: Ist Kultur übersetzbar?* (Kadmos, 2004), *Zone des Übergangs: Vom Ende des Postkommunismus* (Suhrkamp, 2009), *Findet Europa: Eine Suche in der Dolmetscherkabine* (Turia + Kant, 2015), and *Transition to Nowhere: Art in History After 1989* (Archive Books, 2020).

Keti Chukhrov is an art theorist, philosopher, playwright, and poet. Her monograph *Practicing the Good: Desire and Boredom in Soviet Socialism* (University of Minnesota Press, 2020) deals with the impact of socialist political economy on the epistemes of historical socialism. Chukhrov's other books include *To Be—To Perform: "Theatre" in Philosophic Critique of Art* (European Un-ty, 2011), *Pound &£* (Logos, 1999), and a volume of dramatic poems, *Prosto liudi* (Translit–SvobMarxizd, 2010).

Ranjit Hoskote is a poet, cultural theorist, and curator whose work deals with cultural pluralism from the local to the global. He is the author of numerous books, including poetry collections and artist monographs. With Ilija Trojanow, he cowrote *Confluences: Forgotten Histories From East and West* (Yoda Press, 2012). Hoskote has curated, among others, India's first stand-alone pavilion at the Venice Biennale (2011). With Okwui Enwezor and Hyunjin Kim, he cocurated the 7th Gwangju Biennale (2008).

Anton Jäger is a historian of political thought who mainly studies the interrelation between capitalism and democracy, how capitalism both enables and constrains political thinking and acting. His books include *Hyperpolitik: Extreme Politisierung ohne politische Folgen* (Suhrkamp, 2023), *The Populist Moment: The Left after the Great Recession* (with Arthur Borriello, Verso Books, 2023), and *Welfare for Markets: A Global History of Basic Income* (with Daniel Zamora Vargas, The University of Chicago Press, 2023).

Thorsten Mense is a journalist, sociologist, and writer. He has published widely on the resurgence of nationalism in Germany, including the monograph *Kritik des Nationalismus* (Schmetterling, 2016) and the anthology *Rechts, wo die Mitte ist: Die AfD und die Modernisierung des Rechtsextremismus* (coedited with Judith Goetz, Unrast, 2024). In recent years, Mense toured extensively with the multimedia show *Heimat: Eine Besichtigung des Grauens*, codeveloped with Thomas Ebermann and Flo Thamer.

Ingo Niermann is a writer and artist. His meticulous and playful utopias—such as those of *Army of Love* or *Umbauland*—defy established certainties across all ideological camps. His most recent book is *The Monadic Age: Notes on the Coming Social Order* (Sternberg, 2024), a series of thirty-three essays. Together with the artist Erik Niedling, Niermann runs the Documentation Center Thuringia.

Milo Rau is a director and playwright who addresses and reconstructs key moments in recent history and tackles its most controversial problems with an original form of documentary theater. He founded the company International Institute of Political Murder in 2007, and his work has been featured at festivals such as Berliner Theatertreffen, Edinburgh International Festival, Festival d'Avignon, and the Venice Biennale. Between 2018 and 2023, he was the artistic director of NTGent. Since 2024, Rau is the director of the Vienna Festival.

steirischer herbst ’24 Festival Team

Ekaterina Degot
Director and Chief Curator

Rita Puffer
Chief Financial Officer

Theresa Weiler
Director’s Office

David Riff
Senior Curator

Pieternel Vermoortel
Senior Curator

Gábor Thury
Curator

Beatrice Forchini
Assistant Curator

Tobias Ihl
Assistant Curator

Judith Brand
Head of Communications

Georg Hartwig
Press and PR

Martina Heil
Communications

Christina Kasic
Sponsoring/Funding

Fotini Lazaridou-Hatzigoga
Website

Luca Rädler
Communications

Jeff Thoss
Editor

Dietmar Reinbacher
Head of herbst education / Outreach

Lena Kanatschnig
herbst education / Outreach

Vesna Pajičić
herbst education / Outreach

Markus Plasencia
herbst education for Schools

Jakob Schweighofer
Head of Production

Roland Gfrerer
Production

Martin Pelzmann
Production

Karl Masten
Technical Management

Peter Schloss
Exhibition Design

Paulina Maitz
Guest Office

Marlene Obermayer
Head of Archive/Library

Carina Hutter
Archive / Communications /
Curatorial Assistance

Stefanie Lazarus
Office Management

Matthias Ulbl
Personnel/Accounting

Kathrin Lazarus
Personnel/Accounting

Simon Resch
Office Assistant

Danica Radat
Facility Management

Grupa Ee
(Mina Fina, Ivian Kan Mujezinović)
Design

Systemantics
Web Development

Festival Support

Curatorial Department
Lukas Michelitsch

Communications
Henrik Bergstedt
Lesia Goleva
Hannah Klug
Markus Moosbrugger
Sarah Mueller

Visitor Service
Evgeniia Kachmazova
Olgica Perić
Edvin Smajić
Barbara Zambo

Education
Gea Gračner
Laurenz Henkel
Sarah Klaunzer
Evelyn Urban
Paul Wolff

Production
Miriam Bacher
Lukas Bayer
Zoe Borzi
Elsa Chinese
Valentin Hasebe
Lukas Kaiser
Eva Leitner
Heinz Leitner
Ronny Priesching
Eva Schmartschan
Guggi Schneider
Andreas Schögler
Amber Schwinger
Minou Tsambika Polleros

Colophon

This book is published in conjunction with steirischer herbst festival steirischer herbst '24—*Horror Patriae*, September 19–October 13, 2024, Graz, Styria, Austria.

This edition of steirischer herbst was curated by Ekaterina Degot, David Riff, Gábor Thury, and Pieternel Vermoortel, assisted by Beatrice Forchini and Tobias Ihl, and created by all participating artists, speakers, and partner institutions as well as the festival's whole team.

Editors:
Ekaterina Degot
David Riff

With contributions by:
Boris Buden, Keti Chukhrov, Ranjit Hoskote, Anton Jäger, Thorsten Mense, Ingo Niermann, Milo Rau

Managing editor:
Jeff Thoss

Proofreading:
Aaron Bogart

Graphic design and typesetting:
Grupa Ee (Mina Fina, Ivian Kan Mujezinović)

Typefaces:
Mercure
SH24
Studio Pro

Production:
Thomas Lemaître, Hatje Cantz

Printing:
Livonia Print Ltd., Riga

Paper:
Grenita, 250 g/m²
Munken Print White 18, 90 g/m²

steirischer herbst festival gmbh
Sackstraße 17
8010 Graz, Austria
www.steirischerherbst.at

Published by
Hatje Cantz Verlag GmbH
Mommsenstraße 27
10629 Berlin, Germany
contact@hatjecantz.de
www.hatjecantz.com
A Ganske Publishing Group Company

ISBN 978-3-7757-6061-4

Printed in Latvia

Cover illustration:
Grupa Ee